Journey Through the Clouds

Duty, Honor and Country

AS TOLD BY
CARL C. BARNES
WRITTEN BY
ARTHUR H. BARNES

ISBN: 978-1-60414-793-3

Fideli Publishing Inc.
119 W. Morgan St.
Martinsville, IN 46151

www.FideliPublishing.com

For and to Carl:

With the greatest of fondness and respect for the many great memories, plus the love that all brothers should have and share with each other.

Simply proud of Carl,

Art

A Note from Carl C. Barnes:

Some might say it is a dream to walk through life doing what has always been most important to you.

From the earliest memories of my childhood to the greatest moments of my commitment in the field of flight to retirement, I had a dedication to learning and being a part of this most exciting and rewarding endeavor. It was not just a dream.

I am writing this book of my life with my brother in order to let my children and grandchildren know that freedom isn't free. Our freedom today was bought by the blood of millions of service men and women of the military. We had lived through the Depression years. Germany and Japan were trying to take over the world. We were sent to block their takeover, and take back what they had taken. This is just a small part of what I did for my country to help keep it free.

The war years seem so far away from today, but have so marked my emotions and feelings, that they capture the heart of all that I was a part of. The fear and pain of losing comrades that I trained with, shared food and drink with, flew many hours with and then entered combat with only to see them die has traveled with me all these years. I have tried to compress them down to the point where I might forget most of them in the effort to put my trials and tribulations of World War II far out of my mind.

Recalling these events now has awakened much of the sorrow and pain that I experienced so long ago. I am sure recording all that happened will allow a closure of such difficult memories.

My intent to record all of my aviation history herein is my best answer.

Carl C. Barnes, American flyer

An Airman's Prayer

The Lord is my shepherd
I shall be ever grateful.
He guides me through the blue skies
Over the land of the enemies
Even though I fly through the flak and enemy fighters,
I fear the evil and death that is about me for the power of the enemy is great.

Although many will fall from the presence of the enemies,
he will guide me in the paths of his righteousness for his names sake.

Surely, goodness and love will follow me all the days of my life,
and I will dwell in the house of the Lord forever.

Contents

CHAPTER 1

The Youngest Years ... Just Growing Up 1

CHAPTER 2

Art tells the story of 'The Beginning of the Wrong Brothers' 5

CHAPTER 3

The Niche I Never Expected 9

CHAPTER 4

The War Years 13
    POLEBROOK, NORTHAMPTONSHIRE, ENGLAND 13
    POLEBROOK AIR BASE 13
    ABOUT POLEBROOK 14
    MY POSITION AND DUTIES 21
    DOWN TIMES AND CHORES 23
    CONQUERING DOUBTS & FLYING MISSIONS 26
    MISSIONS AND PROBLEMS 28
    DEALING WITH LOSSES AND STRESS 66
    PROCESSED OUT AND HEADED HOME 67
    FINISHING UP 68

CHAPTER 5

A Short Civilian Reprieve 75
    DOMESTIC BLISS 75
    DUTY AND COUNTRY COME CALLING AGAIN 75
    FLYING CARGO 76
    NOT COMBAT, BUT STILL DANGEROUS 78
    STORIES FROM FUKUOKA 78
    BACK TO THE US 81

CHAPTER 6

Civilian Once Again 83
    NORTH AMERICAN AVIATION AND NASA 83
    THE X-15 83
    LIFTING BODIES AND SPACE SHUTTLES 85
    BLACKBIRDS 88
    MAKING AVIATION HISTORY 88
    THE WATER TUNNEL 88
    RECOGNITION 91
    CONCLUSION 100

Bibliography 103

Special Thanks 104

CHAPTER 1

The Youngest Years ... Just Growing Up
1921-1940

According to my birth certificate, I was born in Hugo, Oklahoma on March 10, 1921. My mother was Linnie May Bowen. She was born on May 5, 1900, to Josephine May Pamphlin and Zachary Adam Bowen. We lived in a very marginal farming area with our grandfather; farming mostly cotton, hay and a few other crops.

Later I learned that I had two sisters. The oldest was Velma and next was Shirley. Sometime when I was about six months old, my father decided to move west. With our meager belongings, everything that we owned, we found ourselves in Yuma, Arizona. According to my father's tale, he was broke, with five mouths to feed, no gas for the jalopy and something had to be done.

Dad was one to always find work of some kind and to provide for his family. He soon found work in the fruit orchards and I think that we lived in Yuma for the remainder of the fruit season. Yuma is a very hot dry climate and after the work was over, we piled back into the jalopy and again went west. This time we landed in the Imperial Valley near Banning, California.

Dad found work immediately as foreman in the longer lasting season of California and this lasted thru the remaining season. In about late 1924 or early 1925, Dad's sister, Pearl Winters, wrote that good work could be had in Kern County at a place called Shafter. So off to Shafter we went. Any kind of housing was impossible, so we more or less camped out. Dad went to work right away. All of branches of my family were farmers of one sort or another.

We joined my grandfather farming cotton and alfalfa with the help of our great grandfa-

This is a picture of the Barnes family in Shafter: On the left is my great grandfather, William Cobb Barnes. The stately man in the center is Luther Steve Barnes, my grandfather, then my father, William Milton Barnes. The little guy with no shoes on, and like the big guys in bib overalls, is I. The chickens don't count.

ther. I am glad that I had the farming experience at an early age for it made sure that I didn't want to be a farmer; it was very hard work. Mules were the power for all of the farm equipment and they are stubborn, very stubborn.

On June 14, 1925, my mother, Linnie, died from tuberculosis and was buried in Shafter, California. Taking care of three young kids was an extra burden that was hard for my father, but with the help of my sisters, we did okay.

In early 1926, dad met and courted a young lady named Edith E. Voth. In July 1926, they were married and I found myself with a stepmother. On March 20, 1927, a little late for my birthday, I had a new brother named Arthur.

Somewhere, in about 1927 or 1928, I began my first year of school. This was a country school named Popular located near Shafter. It had all eight grades in one room. Each grade was in a single row and the one teacher would share her teaching from one row to the next. If one of us needed to ask questions, she would usually apologize to the class for interrupting her routine and help the poor stranded student. My time at Popular School was fun and I began the concept of learning.

Dad leased a rather large farm some miles from downtown Bakersfield in 1931. It was part of the family holdings of the Noriga family. Dad farmed about 160 acres, raising mostly cotton, maize and, on one occasion, 20 acres of spinach. He must have been a fan of the comic character Popeye. I remember we tried to eat some of the spinach and the rest went to the cows and pigs.

Shortly after, Dad became restless. He picked up the six of us and moved us to the beautiful val-

When Art, my stepsister Mary and I could bribe Dad, we would ride on his iron-wheeled tractor as he plowed or cultivated the various fields and crops. This was an iron monster, but was the best that he could find. I am on the very front and Art is trying to adjust and Mary maneuver the darned thing. The wheel lugs were heavy wedge like and there must have been 50 of them on each rear wheel.

ley of Ojai, in Ventura County, near the Pacific Ocean. (Ojai is an Indian name for "crow's nest.")

School was a real excitement for me. Grammar school was a snap. High schools challenged me and started my reach for interests that would become my life's vocation. I graduated from Nordoff High School.

Each time an airplane flew over the valley, I'd stare at it until it was out of sight. It seemed impossible for a metal object to stay in the air and move so fast. It wasn't long before I began to make crude models out of soft wood. They were just shapes I saw in my mind, but to me they were airplanes that almost could fly.

I guess Art was close to seven years old then, because he began to bug me about all the things that I did. He wanted me to share some of the craziness with him. He was a patient little guy. I didn't mind explaining what I was doing because he was someone to share it with and he gave me company.

We did things other than airplanes, too. We made some very strange looking kites and carved a weird looking, noisy thing that we swung around our heads from a string or fishing line, if we could find out where Dad kept his fishing gear. It had the shape of a plane fuselage with the tail (vertical stabilizer) carved as part of the device. A carved propeller was fixed to the front.

We would attach the string so that it balanced and then whirl it around our heads. The prop would turn and make a very interesting sound. As soon as I could save enough money, I graduated to a model kit and the serious study and understanding of flight began.

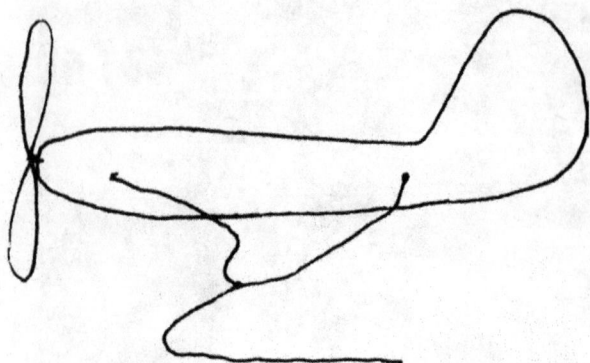

I finished high school in Ojai and worked with my father doing some of the most beautiful stonework that still retains its beauty to this day. He became a Forman of stonemasons, building stone bridges and walls in the greater Ojai Valley.

I guess he got tired of handling the heavy stones, because in about 1937 or 1938, we again moved back to Shafter for several years. Then, in 1940, we moved to Bakersfield, California, where I found what would be the foundation of my life's work.

CHAPTER 2

Art tells the story of
'The Beginning of the Wrong Brothers'
Carl and Art, Ojai, CA — 1934

I enjoyed doing things with Carl, for whatever reason. We did things like making kites, building a tree house, or hunting an imaginary mountain lion along the tall mountains that encompassed the beautiful Ojai Valley, our home.

Carl was the older brother by five years, was not only the leader, but also had an unusual talent as a teacher, an innovator and sharer of his younger brother's ever-inquiring nature. Carl was really my half brother, and I was not just his blind follower; he was a good listener and often made interesting suggestions and I was a contributor to his ever-wandering projects and ideas.

At this particular time, we lived at the bottom of a slight hill just down from a dairy. The hill was most important to the following event. Both Carl and I often took a bucket and obtained fresh milk by trudging up the hill to the dairy, so we became very familiar with that hill. Again, our home was a short distance from the top of the hill and our back door faced down the hill. The back door led to the kitchen.

Carl had an innate attachment to airplanes and the flight of any object. Where this came from, no one can explain. Some of his zeal about airplanes rubbed off on me as we shared wooden models and other flying objects.

Carl was 12 or 13 years old and I was 6 or 7, when Carl decided to build a real, live flying machine — a homemade glider. We cut the tallest and heaviest of the green bamboo poles and with care from the local bamboo stands. We split the bamboo into long thin strips; some of them were 1/2 inch wide, while others were near 1/4-inch in width. They were all cut as long as the poles would allow. After drying, we sanded the strips to remove the fine and troublesome splinters.

Each time we went to the refuse place and to the beach, we scanned for worn-out and discarded beach umbrellas, which we dismantled to retrieve the metal stays that formed the top of the umbrellas. All this effort took most of a year before they had enough supplies to begin the hoped-for flying machine. In order to get my undivided attention and the needed extra hands, Carl promised me a ride on this almost-airplane.

Carl had been collecting every piece of fishing line he could find, even borrowing some from dad's fishing gear when he could. Without any drawings of his planned object, Carl began assembling the body strictly from the image in my mind. I was puzzled about why he was so darned particular about the exact measurements of the different parts of the assembly.

The first part of the assembly was the so-called body or fuselage. It was a triangular mass of struts and ribs that allowed for the flat part of the triangle to become a seat when flying. Then the wings and tail assembly were put together and all were somehow tied together to form the finished extravaganza — an odd looking contraption that looked like *maybe* it could fly.

The putting together was done by tying the strips of bamboo to each other with the fishing line. The stays from the umbrellas became the ribs of the wings. I don't remember what we used for the cloth covering on the wings, but it had to be light and stretched tight across the frame. I'm not sure, but it must have been old bed sheets something similar. Carl did use the proper airplane paint for the coverings, because it was important to have the cloth stretched tight across the ribs and spars of all the air surfaces of the plane. The paint was called airplane "dope" at that time.

After all was completed and ready for flight, we dragged the flimsy craft to the top of the hill that looked down toward the kitchen door of our home. The first flight was filled with great joy and amazement. It really flew!

Gliding not more than 50 or 60 feet above the dairy pasture, it glided down the hill over the dirt road to the dairy. Neighbors were treated to strange sights as they passed the Barnes house in 1934/1935. After a number of flights made only by Carl, with me helping drag the darned thing up the hill and Carl riding it down by himself, I was adamant about the promise of sharing the rides. He finally relented.

The launch procedure involved placing one's fanny astride the triangular fuselage, then holding onto the frame and running as fast as one could to gain airflow over the wings and air surfaces so that flight could begin. Lift and thrust (running) was very real.

Carl put me on the fuselage at the place he judged balance to be correct, then climbed aboard in front of me. With all four of our legs going as fast as they could, down the hill we went.

The gliding or control of the craft was to simply lean left or right to turn the plane or to slide forward or back to control the altitude. All this maneuvering was by "seat of the pants feel," of which only Carl had the knowledge.

Together, the first flight began. As the two of us ran down the hill and lift was achieved, Carl leaned to his right to turn the craft away from our house. I, feeling that I was about to falloff and crash to the ground, naturally leaned to my left to adjust for the feeling of falling.

As we raced with the wind some four to five feet above the descending ground, the kitchen door grew larger and larger. Each time Carl leaned to his right, I leaned further to my left, defeating Carl's ability to turn away from the house and the ever-growing kitchen door.

Let it be noted again, some very basic training on the science of flight and how to control such a craft was most important, and crash procedures should have been thoroughly reviewed. Carl had always been good at sharing the "how to" of his inventions. I thought the emotions of the great art of flying distracted Carl from this very important function.

Regardless, down the crest of the hill, down the slope, and on we went, feet pounding faster and faster down the hill. A good wind caught the wings and lift was acquired. Carl leaned right and I unintentionally, through lack of training, corrected Carl's attempts to turn.

There was a sound of splintering wood as we crashed straight through the kitchen door. With the door laying torn from its hinges and pieces of broken bamboo, cloth and fishing line strewn allover the kitchen floor, my mother, in the final stages of preparing dinner, very calmly turned and said, "Wait until your father gets home!"

So ended the early careers of two very young would-be aviators. Their hurt pride in losing the flying machine and the sure-to-be physical reprimand when father got home took away most of the joy gained from flight. We cleaned up the remains of our plane and talked about what went wrong as we waited for our father.

For and to Carl:

With the greatest of fondness and respect for the many great memories, plus the love that all brothers should have and share with each other.

Simply proud of you!
Art

CHAPTER 3

The Niche I Never Expected
DREAMS COMING TRUE

There was an opening for a young guy to service the airplanes coming and going Kern County Airport. My first real paying job!

The airport had a fuel pit with a long hose and I would refuel the planes as requested. Most of them were small planes that required starting the engine by pulling the propeller to crank the engine. This cranking also became my job. I was not a big guy, but I still had to do it.

One Sunday, a Navy amphibian-type plane, (the first I had seen) came onto the field. It was a monster — a biplane with a big pontoon with wheels that folded up into the pontoon. Of course, the wheels came down for landing on a runway. The plane landed and required refueling with 100-octane aviation gas. The pilot then wanted me to "crank-start" the engine.

He described how I was to crawl out along the fuselage on some small steps between the two wings and turn a crank to wind it up to a high pitch. The engine had an inertial-type starter. One could crank and crank, making it go faster and faster. When the starter was at a scream, I would get down and the pilot would pull the engage lever in the cockpit with the engine starting to turn over.

I did this about three times and it didn't start. I gave up, but the pilot kept on saying, "Okay, buddy. Just one more time. Just one more time." Boy, the cranking really pooped me out! I got up one more time, cranked my heart out until the scream became a high pitch. The pilot pulled the lever and the engine started with a roar. The pilot quickly taxied out to the runway and took off. Was I glad to see him go!

In late 1940 or early 1941, the government established a pilot training school at the Kern County Airport to train American would-be

The air academy had several different types of trainers for the Eagle Squadron trainees to fly. The primary trainers were several PT-17s, a bi-wing fabric, two-seat, do-everything plane. This was the first plane on which a student began his instruction.

After the required hours in the PT -17, and if the student passed his test, he would graduate to the BT-13, a basic trainer, shown above in the air and below on the ground. It had an enclosed cockpit, all metal frames and more horsepower.

aviators for the British Air Force. These pilots were known as the Eagle Squadron. The school was just becoming stable when WWII broke out. I had gone to work for them as a mechanic and was learning a great deal that would earn me a government certified aviation mechanic ticket (A&E).

Part of my responsibility was the overall maintenance of the PT-17 trainers, which included every facet of mechanical needs from engine change to fixing a bad tire. On occasion, I would get a check ride. If the instructor were a good guy, he would let me handle the controls, but not a landing. The training area was all around Kern County on general training, and as the pilots

became competent, they would begin cross-country flights.

The last plane for their final training was the North American AT-6 trainer. It had retractable landing gear and a much more powerful engine. There were times that the fledgling pilots would forget a few items, especially upon landing.

During our flight training at Imperial Airport, we lost our first pilot. He had completed his final solo and was on a night flight. For reasons unknown, he crashed his AT-6 in the center of one of the country roads. The recovery task, cleaning up the residue of the plane, was a real eye-opener for me. Investigators went thru the site with fine-toothed combs trying to learn the cause of the crash. None was found. There was a very sobering attitude around the field for several months after the crash.

For some reason the problems always occurred with the AT-6s. During the next incident, the pilot did not lower his landing gear. When he was asked, "Didn't you hear the tower calling?"

His response was, "I couldn't hear a darned thing because a horn was making so much noise."

The senior pilot informed the student that the "horn" was an emergency sound to let the student know he had to lower his gear. As a reminder, the errant pilot might be given the punishment of walking for several hours with his parachute banging him in his legs.

On another occasion, the pilot thought he was running out of runway and really set down hard on his brakes. As a result, the plane stood on end with the propeller dug deep into the runway. I think that is where the term "cockpit trouble" was born.

In 1941, the Kern County Airport was taken over by the U.S. Army Air Force. After that, B-17s and some P-40s came roaring onto the field. The U.S. was at war with Japan.

The school didn't last long at the Kern County Airport. It was transferred lock stock and planes to El Centro, California and the Imperial County Airport while a new facility was under construction some 15 miles west.

It was winter when we were at El Centro and the weather was not too bad. Again, the school, Plosser and Prince Air Academy, was getting everything under control with the move from Bakersfield when the Navy decided to takeover the new field. They claimed it was just what they needed to train Navy pilots in advanced flying.

Packing our bags and planes once again, this time the move was to Texas — Sweetwater, Texas (somewhat in the middle of nowhere). The field was named Avenger Field and was about 10 miles west of the town. It was totally new with quality barracks and some decent hangars.

At first, the primary trainers, PT-17 Stearmans, were managed from a steel Quonset-type building that had been the main hanger before the new facilities were built. It was kind of funny in a way. As the instructor and student departed the ready ramp, they had to go down a reasonable

slant to the taxiway. I always waited for one of the new students to clamp down on the brakes and set the plane on its nose, but it never happened.

The BT-13s and AT-6s were managed across the field in the new hangars and classrooms.

Avenger became a very busy field. The classes increased and the constant takeoffs and landings

STEARMAN PT-13A PRIMARY TRAINER
U.S. ARMY AIR CORPS

Carl Barnes

became routine. I'd become crew chief by this time and spent almost all my time on the AT-6 aircraft.

One day when it was my turn to pick up the mail, I was called over to an Army Air Force officer who was just outside the post office and he gave me a real rush about the Air Force and flying. When he found out where I was working and my experience, he was ready to get me in the Air Force. When I returned to Avenger Field, I was in the Army Air Force and had just two weeks to put my personal stuff together. Then it was off to flight school.

WRITERS NOTE: *Avenger Field became the training center for the Woman's Ferry command pilots. Many of our great lady pilots passed thru this field.*

Chapter 4

The War Years

DUTY HONOR COUNTRY
1942—1945

POLEBROOK, NORTHAMPTONSHIRE, ENGLAND

When the 351st Bomb Group was formed, there were so few crews and planes available that each Squadron was formed into 6 B-17s in each Squadron. As more crews completed training and planes were available, the individual Squadrons were changed to 4 planes in each box. Again, more crews and more planes flew to the combat zone they were again changed to 12 planes in each Squadron, which formed a Squadron box. Within a Squadron, each plane flew about 50 feet from the lead plane and each box then flew at a different altitude from the lead box. This gave the group some 34-50 Caliber machine guns for defense

POLEBROOK AIR BASE

Arrival at the Polebrook Army Air Force base did not mean that our crew was ready to begin our missions over Germany. There was a lot of new training to be done and our aircraft commander was required to make a mission as co-pilot with another crew that had flown several missions into Germany's front yard.

Our crew thought that we had been over trained before we left the states, but so near battle, we had to learn new bail-out procedures that let us know how serious the war really was. First, we couldn't wear our parachutes while manning our battle stations. In order to fly the plane or fire our weapons, our chutes were stored as close to our station as possible. Should we get hit in an area where fuel was stored, the plane would surely be on fire. We had only a few seconds to evacuate the plane before it exploded into a thousand pieces. *(This did happen often, with the plane's crew blown to pieces.)*

Formation flying was another different drill. Each plane in the formation had to fly as close to the other planes in their squadron as possible — less than 50 feet wing tip to wing tip. The dire need was for the protection of all planes in the group. More guns to bear on an enemy attack were mandatory if a crew was to get back to the base. A B-17 outside of the group was a major target for any attacking German fighter.

Something else none of us had thought about was, "What if we're shot down?" Each crewmember had a passport-type photo taken where we were wearing typical French, Belgium or other European-type clothing. The thought was that if we were stopped by the Germans and asked questions, the passport at least made it look like we were European. Each of us was given, as part of our flight kit, a survival package that included money from several different countries and some papers stating a possible occupation or work skill. Every effort was made to give us a small measure of stuff that would help us get to the underground or escape on our own if our crew was shot down.

French passport photo.

ABOUT POLEBROOK

The 351st Bomb Group's base was some 60 miles north and west of the great city of London and not far from Peterborough, the nearest town of any size. Peterborough was also our best liberty destination.

We shared the base with the night bombing groups of the RAF wings. They flew their missions over Germany at night and we flew during the daylight hours. There were always plenty of comings and goings of heavy bombers.

Our only after-flight watering hole and relaxing place was a "pub" about two miles down a sometimes-paved road. The pub sat like a farmhouse in the country.

Each evening there were always various members of the different squadrons, both flight and ground personnel, getting away from it all at the pub. There were a lot of air combat tales being told. Things like how one gunner shot down several Messerschmitt 109s or a Fockewulfs German fighter on his last mission, and as usual, another gunner claiming that he was the one who shot down at least one of the bragged-about scores. There were always a lot of great tales to share with each squadron, especially after a mission, and as always, the humble and painful loss of one or more of the B-17s on the day's mission.

The sorrow and pain was thick when one of the older flight crews that may have had only one or two more missions to complete their 35 flights into hell was lost.

On a happier note, many of the lost crews were successful in returning to England.

During our first introduction upon arriving at Polebrook, the base commander scared the living hell out of us. He began by letting us know that some 125 percent of all the crews so far had been shot down. He said we might be able to make about 16 of the 35 missions, if we were lucky. Further, as he detailed our probable future, he said we might as well consider ourselves dead as of that moment.

I don't remember if I had any feelings left after that first meeting or not. Here I was a 20-year-old with feelings of duty, honor and country that had never seen a German, and I was to think I was "dead"?

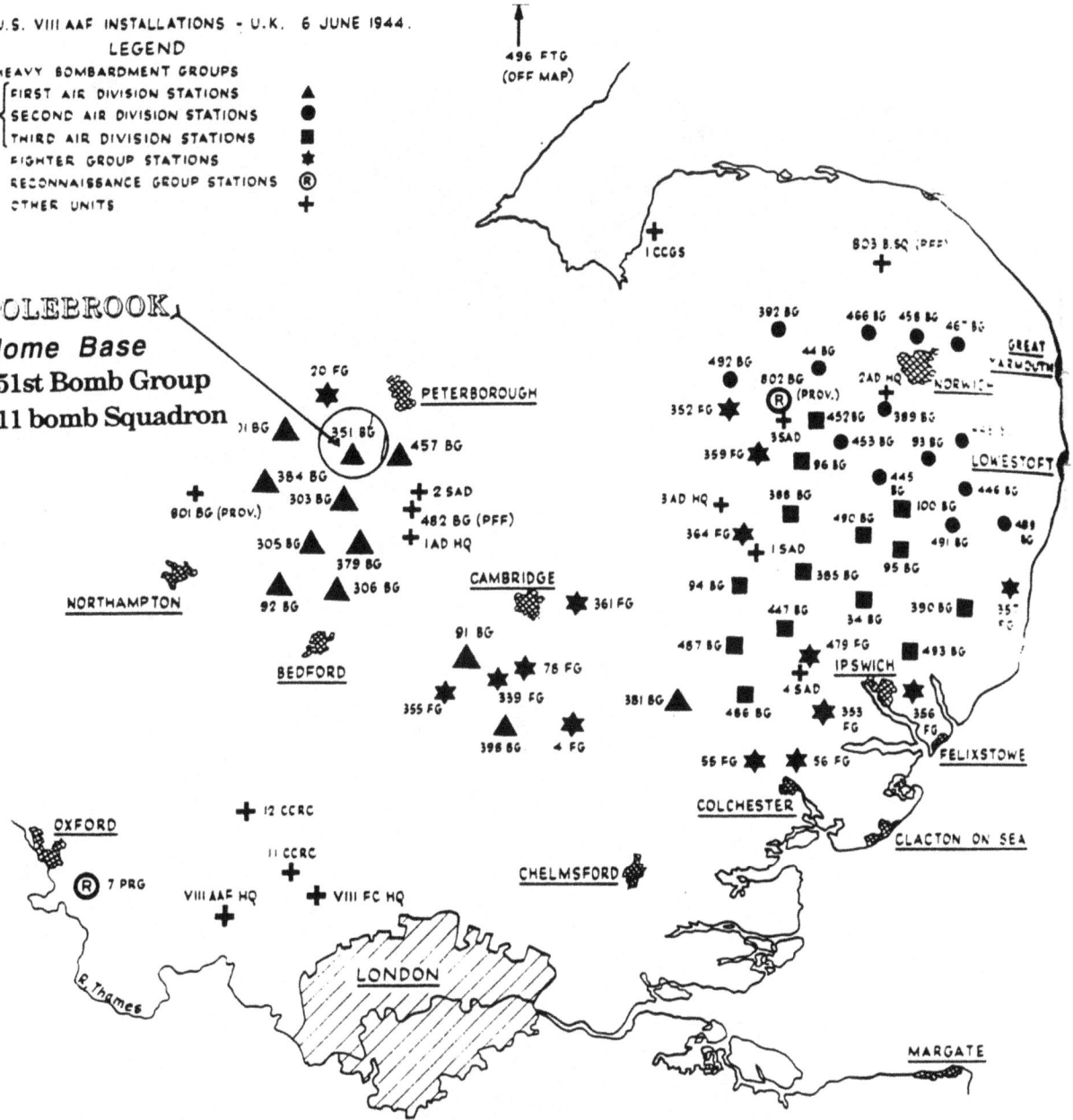

U.S. VIII AAF INSTALLATIONS - U.K. 6 JUNE 1944.
LEGEND

HEAVY BOMBARDMENT GROUPS
FIRST AIR DIVISION STATIONS ▲
SECOND AIR DIVISION STATIONS ●
THIRD AIR DIVISION STATIONS ■
FIGHTER GROUP STATIONS ★
RECONNAISSANCE GROUP STATIONS ®
OTHER UNITS ✛

POLEBROOK
Home Base
351st Bomb Group
511 bomb Squadron

Unit	Location	Equipment	Unit	Location	Equipment
VIII AAF HQ	HIGH WYCOMBE		96 BG	SNETTERTON HEATH	B-17
VIII FC HQ	BUSHEY HALL		100 BG	THORPE ABBOTTS	B-17
1AD HQ	BRAMPTON GRANGE		303 BG	MOLESWORTH	B-17
2AD HQ	KETTERINGHAM HALL		305 BG	CHELVESTON	B-17
3AD HQ	ELVEDEN HALL		306 BG	THURLEIGH	B-17
4 FG	DEBDEN	P-51	339 FG	FOWLMERE	P-51
7 PRG	MOUNT FARM	F-5	351 BG	POLEBROOK	B-17
20 FG	KINGS CLIFFE	P-38	352 FG	BODNEY	P-47
34 BG	MENDLESHAM	B-24	353 FG	RAYDON	P-47
44 BG	SHIPDHAM	B-24	355 FG	STEEPLE MORDEN	P-51
55 FG	WORMINGFORD	P-38	356 FG	MARTLESHAM HEATH	P-47
56 FG	BOXTED	P-47	357 FG	LEISTON	P-51
78 FG	DUXFORD	P-47	359 FG	EAST WRETHAM	P-47
91 BG	BASSINGBOURN	B-17	361 FG	BOTTISHAM	P-47
92 BG	PODINGTON	B-17	364 FG	HONINGTON	P-38
93 BG	HARDWICK	B-24	379 BG	KIMBOLTON	B-17
94 BG	BURY ST EDMUNDS	B-17	381 BG	RIDGEWELL	B-17
95 BG	HORHAM	B-17	384 BG	GRAFTON UNDERWOOD	B-17

15

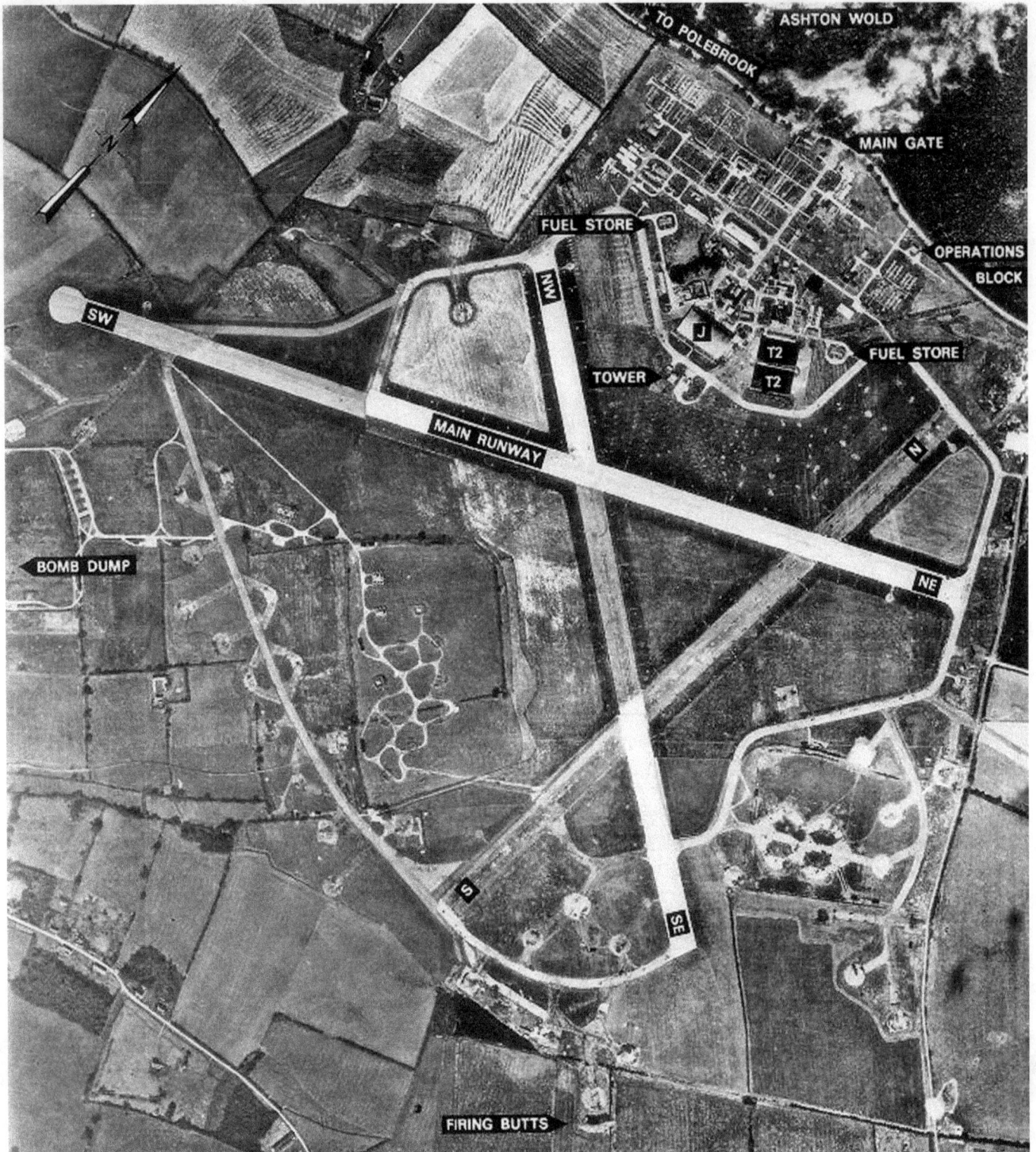

1943 Polebrook overhead view

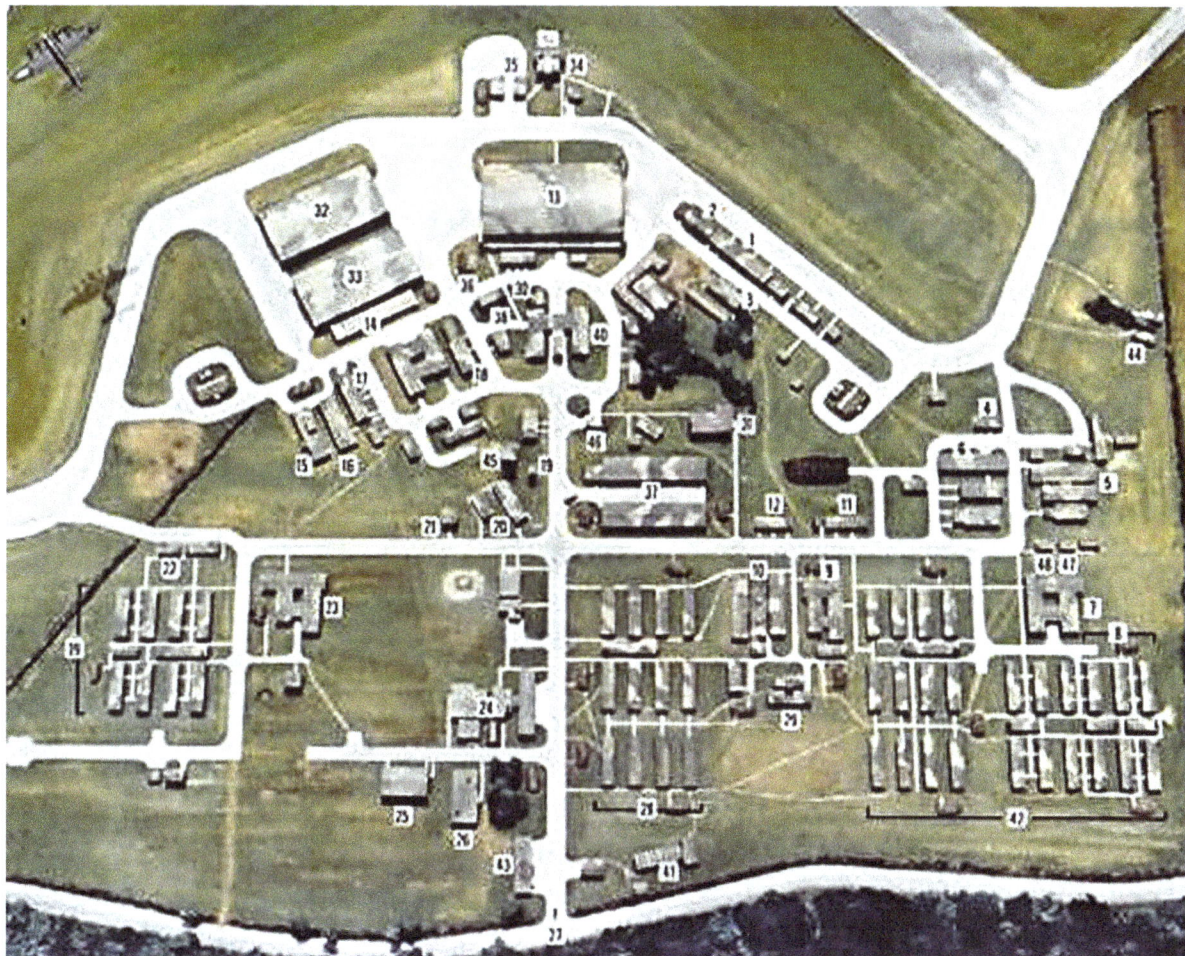

1. 509th Squadron Operations
2. Main Briefing Room
3. 509th Drying Room & Equipment Bldg.
4. 509th Orderly & Mail Room
5. Nav Room & Gp Equipment Bldg. (Dinghy Drill)
6. Hospital
7. Officers Club & Mess (Combat)
8. Officers B.O.Q. (509th Sq.)
9. Sergeants Club
10. Enlisted Men's Mess
11. P.X.
12. Post Office & Barber Shop
13. Main Hangar (American Trainer)
14. Gp Gunnery Office - (Communications Office)
15. 509th Armament Office
16. 510th Armament Office
17. 508th Armament Office
18. Photo Lab
19. AML Trainer Bldg.
20. Link Trainer Bldg.
21. Spotlight Trainer Bldg.
22. Cleaning & Laundry - Officers only
23. Staff Officers Mess
24. Group Headquarters
25. Gym
26. Church Army
27. Main Gate
28. E.M. Barracks (Combat)
29. 509th Supply Room
30. Flak Suits
31. Polebrook Lodge (Special Services - Library)
32. Auxiliary Hangar (A)
33. Auxiliary Hangar (B)
34. Control Tower
35. Fire Trucks - Garage
36. Welding Shop
37. Motor Pool
38. Parachute Shop
39. Officers Quarters (Ground)
40. Automotive Main Shop
41. M.P. Barracks
42. Flightcrews Barracks
43. Guard House O.D.
44. Sheet Metal Building
45. Water Tower Weather Man
46. Bomb Site Bldg.
47. 510th Orderly Room
48. 511th Orderly Room

I do remember that as the crew gathered after the meeting there was a lot of inner struggle to conquer the desire to go home to the USA, *now!*

We'd had over a year of total training and about one year of that was with our crew. We had flown together as one, slept in the same barracks, eaten the same food, shared liberty, talked about our families and hometowns, and in general bonded and become closer than most family members. We had to depend upon each other in a way that was literally life or death. Maybe it was the way things were going to be.

Getting around the base and also down to the pub was by bicycle. When a crew had experienced its 35 missions or the loss of a crewmate, it was a prize to take over or outbid for their two-wheeler. It seemed there were never enough

Our pilot, McMamaar, and Bombardier, Mishkin, liked to goof around like all the rest of the crew. It was good that Mishkin was a slight person because riding on the front wheel made it easier for the pilot to "fly" the bike.

bikes to go around for those who needed them. The bikes were a treasure to those who were lucky enough to own one, since the base was so scattered out that it was impossible to get around without a one.

Officers as well as the enlisted crews had the same problem. The ground crew usually had a truck or Jeep for transportation. The officers were not as aggressive as some of the enlisted flyers and at times would double up on a bike to get around. I was amazed that with all the flying, the crews could find time and freedom to just fool around and have what seemed to be fun.

During non-flying days, which were few, there seemed to be time for casual moments of entertainment. When a camera was available,

Carl Barnes on his bike on base.

Some of our crew in a more casual moment. Left is our navigator, R. L. Arceneaux. He was from Louisiana and had one of the best attitudes of the officers. He joked around a lot. One the right is our very front guy, H.M. Mishkin, the bombardier. His home was Long Island and when he said, "Bombs away!" they were always right on the target. Mishkin also manned the front chin turret that had two 50-caliber machine guns. Arceneaux manned the two single 50-caliber guns referred to as cheek guns. They pointed out from each side of the fuselage and had a fixed point of aim. Both positions fired at an oncoming enemy fighter with great skill.

photos were taken of different members of our crew — both air and ground.

As soon as we were assigned a plane, our ground crew began the routine of making sure the plane was in first class flying condition. We couldn't fly a lot of days because of the weather.

During these weather breaks, I got to where I could play chess pretty well. I read a lot of books and we would go over to the service club and

play the jukebox and listen to Bing Crosby sing "I'm Dreaming of a White Christmas."

Well, we had a white Christmas, but it wasn't something you would dream about. One day we went down and decided to do some skeet shooting and practice up on shooting fighters. That's what it was for, to keep you in practice. We went down to the skeet range, checked out our shotguns, shells and some skeet. First time we fired, a cluster of pheasants flew up and we whammed them, killed a couple of them and grabbed them up.

The monkey sitting on Armstrong's shoulders belonged to a little old organ grinder. Armstrong was our Copilot and sat in the right seat of the cockpit. To the left is our radio operator, E. A. Baron, late of Toledo, Ohio. He sat in the center of the plane in a space all by himself. It was full of radio equipment that was important for intercom and also for group and main base communication if the weather closed in with fog. Mishkin, on the right, seemed to be around with the crew most of the time. Armstrong was from the great state of Texas, and he never let us forget it.

The skeet range was close to an Englishman's house, and he came running out and said, "You can't do that. Those are the king's birds."

We replied, "The king said it was okay."

He replied, "Oh, no you didn't talk to him. You've never seen the king."

We quickly jumped on our bikes with our two pheasants and peddled back to our barracks with him right behind us. We ran into the barracks, went around back and hid the pheasant under the barracks.

The Englishman went into the office and complained to the first sergeant that we were out shooting "the king's birds." The first sergeant had to do his job. So he came into the barracks with the limey. We were sitting there nonchalantly reading magazines like nothing had happened.

The limey pointed to us and said, "They shot the king's birds! They shot the king's birds!"

The first sergeant looked at him and said, "Where's your evidence?"

The Englishman looked around and couldn't find even a feather. The sergeant said, "Well, we have no evidence. We can't prove it." The limey left, chattering to himself. The first sergeant went on back and kinda winked. He knew what had happened.

As soon as he left, we went around and jerked those birds out and cleaned them up. We went to the mess tent and got some butter. We took our mess kits out and fried them birds out. They were kinda tough, but knowing we stole those birds from the king, they tasted pretty good.

Of course, the officers had their own barracks where two persons shared one room. Their "chow hall" was separate from the enlisted crewmembers as well. Their barracks was titled "Sack Happy Shack, Section 8." It was no better than the building that housed the enlisted crew. It had the same coal-burning stove. They did have one advantage —a servant (an enlisted man) to keep the coal bin filled and the fire always burning.

Behind our living quarters there was a woods. There were a lot of tree squirrels out there. The tail gunner made himself a slingshot and would go out and shoot the squirrels, and then bring them in and cook them. He was an old country boy from Nebraska. The English called them tree rats.

Other afternoons when there wasn't a flight we would ride the bus into Peterborough. When we'd get off the bus there was always a bunch of kids standing around saying, "Got some gum, chum?" or "Got some candy, Andy?" You could go through a pack of gum really quick. So, we bought some Chiclets and would give them out.

The one who kept her in fine tune day in and day out was the crew chief and his two skilled mechanics. Before a flight, the crew chief would turn over all of the paperwork

Navigator ARC.

We had several different specialists who made repairs to the plane's damage after a mission. The names have escaped me, but their faces are a part of our gratitude for their painstaking attention to our plane before and after each mission.

that covered problems from the previous flight and a complete list of the fuel on board to the flight engineer, and he would receive the list of men that were making the flight that day.

The crew chief had a tent-like office just to the rear of the plane's hardstand and he spent all of his time on the plane or in his so-called office. It was an unheated place that was never warm, day or night. Most of the work on the plane was done at night. In England, there were very few warm days.

MY POSITION AND DUTIES

My mission requirements started as soon as I could get to the plane. First, the ground chief would give me his repair or fixes of the "squawks" from the previous flight and we would discuss their status. He would also tell me the number of rounds of 50-caliber ammo he'd put on board and the fuel amount. I sometimes questioned him about the fuel because he had loaded the maximum. I would ask him how he knew that we

Flight and maintenance crew, Polebrook.

I have saved the best for last, at least from my point of view. I was the best. Carl C. Barnes, Chief Flight Engineer. The "glass house" that my hand is resting against was my domain when the shooting started. It housed twin 50-caliber machine guns and was part of a 360-degree turning turret. I just barely had room to stick my head into the dome to fire. Each gun's breech mechanism was all but touching both my ears. When I fired the thing, even with earphones on, I could not hear anything but the chatter of the guns firing. I had headaches from the noise when we encountered many German fighters and I had to fight them off over a long period.

were going on a long mission. His simple answer was, "I knew before you did."

I had paperwork to complete before we could fly. One of the most important items was the crew list. Each crewmember had to be listed by full name, serial number and rank. When a plane did not return, it was mandatory to have this completed list in order to know who was missing.

At the end of a mission, I also had to hand over a list of new squawks noted on that mission to the ground chief. Bullet holes and flak holes did not count. There was a special crew with a long semi-truck that had everything needed to patch all the smaller holes. Their chief would examine the plane and count the holes, plus mark each hole with a colored marker.

The trailer crew had patches of aluminum cut to fit the many different sized holes. They would cut away all the torn metal, slap one of the precut patches over the hole and rivet it into place. Quick and dirty, but it would do the job.

It was also my job to sit just aft of the pilot during takeoff and landing to assist him should there be a need. There was never a lack of important things to do.

DOWN TIMES AND CHORES

There is a sort of love for the B-17 from each of the crewmates. When I could not dampen my ever-growing fright of a next mission, I would take my bicycle and rove about the base, checking on the status of our plane. It was also a chance to plane talk with the chief ground engineer and learn some of the problems that he and his crew had in keeping the ship flying.

At times he would admit that when he signed the plane ready to fly, he had his doubts about it making it. His comment, "The old gal has taken so darned many bad beatings I wonder how she makes it each time your guys go out. You could never get me to fly in any one of them that has been flying as long as your plane." We had no choice; it was the only one we had.

After so many missions, we were given a pass to take in London for several days. The one time we went to London, we were almost killed by a raiding German bomber. We found another nice town that was as far from the "Battle of Britain" as we could get for future leaves. … It was in Scotland!

When we had a break from flying combat missions, some of us would have several days leave. Scotland was a popular destination for all of the crews. A train ride of several hours would let us get far away from the constant enemy bombing and the flights of the German V-1 and V-2 rocket attacks. Closer to the fighting, one could never tell when one of the crazy things

Bagpiper in Inverness.

would come over and there was no, or little warning, especially with the V-2.

After 25 missions, a crew was given a week of R&R (rest and recreation). You could go to different houses where you could go and just eat and sleep. A couple of us guys in our crew decided to go to Edinburgh up in Scotland for the week so we could see things. It was more relaxing to go out and see part of Scotland.

The Red Cross would make arrangements with different families that would take servicemen in for a small payment per day. They would give you breakfast and a bed.

We went through the big castle there where we saw lots of armor suits standing around in dif-

ferent places. There were old fellas in there that would show you around. The waist gunner saw a suit of armor there and said, "Man, what a great flak suit that would be. I gotta find me one to fit."

One of the old guys overheard and said, "You can't take 'em, you know."

Ralph said, "Sure. I need to find one that fits." The waist gunner had been hit several times by flak, so the suit looked really good to him.

He made the old guy worry. He kept an eye on him the whole time we were there, thinking he would steal one of those suits of armor.

Our Scot visits were always ones of relaxing and letting our personal fears subside somewhat. Just walking through some of the small towns and speaking the Gaelic language, or trying to, was a great diversion from the war.

The sharing of an evening in one of their pubs, even though I was not a drinking person, was more than a delight. The locals were so grateful for our (American) presence in the war, it was very difficult to spend a dime (farthing). My memories still bring a feeling of warmth at their friendship.

We saw quite a bit of Edinburgh and went to dances at night. I met this gal, an American nurse, who was a captain, I think. She asked, "Would you like to have a steak?"

I said, "A steak. What's that?"

She said, "Don't you know what a steak is?"

I replied, "I've been there long enough that I can't figure out what a steak is anymore."

She said to follow her and we went into a pub. She spoke to the bartender there and we around the bar and into the back room, and then ordered a steak.

We got steak and potatoes. It was a steak, but I still think it was a horse steak. It was so tough you could hardly chew it. But it looked like a steak, anyway.

We rented a taxi for the day and he took us all around Edinburgh. That week went fast.

Several times when there was a no fly day, some of the different crews sat around our mealtime tables and listened to crewmembers telling of the latest missions. On one occasion, our crew was sharing a table with a crew that had just completed their third mission. They were commenting on how rough it was. Several of our crew joined in by asking, "Really? Was it that rough?"

It was habit of each crew to list their number of missions on the back of their flight jackets, with the bomb missions indicated by bombs in groups of five. When our crew had listened to enough, we got up and started to walk away with our 25 missions showing clearly on the back of our jackets. The three-mission crew just gasped in amazement as we departed.

It was difficult for them to understand how any crew could survive many more missions like the one they were describing, let alone 25 missions facing death over German cities. When I thought about it, it was hard for me to understand just how we had survived that many. There had to be a higher power riding in our plane.

Personal chores were another problem. Who likes to do their laundry in the cold fog, or worse, the rain? Each barracks had a simple wash table for cleaning clothes with basic dirt. When it came to oil-soaked work gear, any kind of cleaning fluid was used. Aviation gas was the easiest to find and, as such, became the leading fluid of choice. There were enough examples of where not to use the gas, so it was always done in the open air, away from everything.

There was often a movie at a makeshift theatre, but it was always cold so not many of the crew attended. The pub about a mile down the road was the preferred spot to hang out. It was

I had to have some kind of souvenir from a clan. A photo was the best way. I would like to note, my heritage was Scottish, so it was not out of character to don the colors, even if I was not sure of my historical past.

always warm and full of aircrews and ground guys. It was the closest thing to home we had, and that's saying a lot.

Polebrook was located about ten miles from a number of other B-17 bases. Meetings at the pubs offered a chance to learn how some of the other bomb groups were faring. The one pub I remember most was the one about a mile down the road. It was called "Oundle."

On one of our missions over Hanover, #18, we had really taken a beating from the German fighters. We had two engines shot out and were just barely flying at wave-top level across the channel. We were over an hour late getting back.

Debriefing took some time and my paperwork took more. I had a date with a nice lady at the pub and some of my best "buddies" had told her I'd been shot down. They, of course, moved in on my date.

As I walked into the pub, she jumped up and screamed, "You lied! You lied!" to my buddy and then she ran to me and gave me one of the best hugs I'd ever gotten from her. There *are* some rewards at times.

CONQUERING DOUBTS & FLYING MISSIONS

I am not sure just when I started counting the number of missions left and had a strong feeling that I would not be around long enough to make 35. I think it was somewhere between mission 5 and 6 that the reality of being shot down became a constant part of my daily thoughts.

Each morning before a flight, around 0130 (1:30 a.m.), one of the ground staff would come into our barracks and wake each crew that was designated to fly that day. After a while, I noticed he had a reluctant tone to his voice. When I had a chance to ask him about it, he replied that it was difficult waking a mission of airmen knowing there would be empty bunks that evening. Even though he did not fly with them, he was an equal part of the wing and hurt just the same way.

"You see, Carl," he said to me, "I make the same bonded friends that the air crews do and, in some cases, I become very close to one or two of the flying crew. When they do not return, I cry the same as you and the other crewmembers. It really hurts to see such a waste of young men." When I had time to think about what he had said, I was sympathetic the next time he came calling our crew.

After struggling awake, the crew would gather up our flight gear, and slowly make our way to the mess hall for breakfast. There was not a great deal of conversation during breakfast since each member was thinking about what he'd face in the next 12 or so hours.

There was a set time for mission briefings for all crews that were to fly so we could learn where we would face death that day. I could already begin to see the hundreds of black puffs of flak and the darting Messerschmitt 109s and Fockewulfs German fighters coming at us. Even the sound of the B-17s' engines crept into my mind.

When you have flown the many hours our crew had, there are not too many sounds of the flight that everyone is not well attuned to. If the pilot made the slightest change in propeller pitch or changed the throttle setting, it was felt and noted. All that was going on made life extremely special, but for many, exceedingly short.

After we learned where our mission was for that day, we were trucked out to our waiting aircraft. It stood like so many others — staggered along a taxiway so that any surprise German attack would destroy just a few. Each member of the crew went to his respective combat station and began to check out the guns, radio, plane's controls and set the bombsight in place.

The plane commander would call out all the crew for a report of readiness. Sometimes, we would just sit on the tarmac waiting for the signal to start engines. This usually happened when the weather prevented immediate lineup and takeoff.

The plane's brakes would be released and with the roar of the engines, we surged down the runway. The roll began slowly for the plane since crew, fuel and bomb load made the B-17's total weight many tons.

The crew could feel the rumble of the tires as our plane picked up speed and the airflow across the plane's surfaces began to take hold. There was always a prayer that a tire would not blow out or an engine would not fail — basically that nothing would go wrong during the takeoff effort. We could feel when the plane was ready to fly.

Some of the ground effect would diminish and the efforts of the pilot to fly the plane off the runway would become apparent. The plane would then leave the ground and all the rumbling noise would stop. A slight wiggle of the plane's controls and the pilot took over complete command of the flight.

The nose would tilt up slightly due to the heavy load and we would start our climb. We waited for the sound of the flaps being retracted and the thump of the landing gear as it locked into its housings.

It was also a tense moment before we cleared the fog or overcast as we began to reach the join-up position for the group's course to the target. The waist gunners rechecked their 50-caliber machine guns and the ammunition; the tail gunner would announce that he had done his checking. The ball gunner folded his body down into his round Plexiglas domain where everything that might come at us was his target.

The ball gunner was holed up in a dome-like ball underneath the center of the fuselage. He was more or less stuffed inside and could swivel his turret in all directions covering the underside of the plane. He could also warn the crew of fighters that seemed to delight in attacking from

below. Our ball gunner was G. S. Cluett from New York.

As crew chief, I was responsible for making sure the crew was at their respective stations and had all the required items for defending us. I was also on hand to manage the flight controls should that be needed.

Calls sometimes came in from the different crew positions that a B-17 had broken through the fog or overcast and was moving to take up its position in the group. This was a reassuring moment because it meant we would be flying with a number of planes close by rather than scattered across the sky. The tighter the group, the better security was for all the planes.

As we came close to enemy territory, each man check-fired his gun and reported. My combat position was the top gun turret, which had two 50-caliber machine guns mounted side by side with the major part of the gun inside the dome. This barely gave me room for my head and the visual sight that allowed me to aim and fire the darned thing.

This position also gave me the best view of anyone or anything that would be coming from above. The German fighters liked to dive on the B-17s, so I had the best view to warn our crew that trouble was at hand and begin tracking the target ready to fire as they came within range.

I also had the best view of the flak. The Germans sent it up and it exploded above the plane. The ball turret gunner had the best view of the flak that exploded below the plane. Regardless, when the flak began, everyone on the crew knew it and additional fear set in.

As the flak exploded, the shell would fly into many pieces headed in all directions. If this happened close enough, it would put a hole in the plane as big as the piece of flak hitting the plane. If it hit a vital place, a great deal of damage would result. Of course, if one of the crew was hit, well, you can only guess the deep concern that everyone had.

Each mission followed this basic pattern. The only difference was the type of target and the German determination to defend it. The more important the target, the better it was defended and the more dangerous the mission.

MISSIONS AND PROBLEMS

Each mission had its problems, from starting engines to touchdown after a mission. As hard as the ground force tried, they often would have at least one plane that was not going to fly that day. A standby plane was always part of each mission. If a plane had to turn back, the standby plane simply filled in.

When the roll for takeoff began, each plane thereafter would roll every 30 seconds, staggering in the prop wash of the plane in front. It was a great chore for the pilot to keep control as the plane climbed out to join formation. On more than one occasion, a plane would overtake or slide too far out of line and crash into the plane in front or alongside it. Fuel and bombs would let the next in line know that a major tragedy had taken place and that there would be empty bunks in the barracks that night.

As our flight made their formation, and the crew settled down at their battle stations, the main effort was from our plane's navigator, R. L. Arceneaux. Almost immediately, the pilot called out, "Where are we, navigator? Don't get us lost." It was McMamarr's way to let the navigator know that he wanted to get to the target and home with as little fuss as possible.

When flying in a large formation, there was always a lead navigator who was responsible for the correct approach to the target for the whole group. When we had the lead, which was every

fourth mission, "Arc" did the navigating and never missed the target

The navigator also had another duty. On each side of the fuselage was a single 5-caliber machine gun. These guns had fixed positions so that they could not be aimed, they just fired forward at an enemy plane coming directly towards them. Each gun had a special ammunition belt that was fixed so that it did not get in the way of either the bombardier or the navigator. Altogether, the forward part of the nose of the plane was pretty cramped.

As a flight made the formation and headed to the target, most of the crew calmed down somewhat. That usually lasted for about 15 minutes. As we crossed the English Channel, and in some cases were in enemy territory, a tenseness and fear would return as each crew member made a final check and the gunners test-fired their 50-caliber machine guns.

Looking out over the flight at high altitude, we could easily see our path by the vast white contrails. Each plane left a form of ice as it flew. The heat from our aircraft engine in the very cold altitude caused the effect and also let the

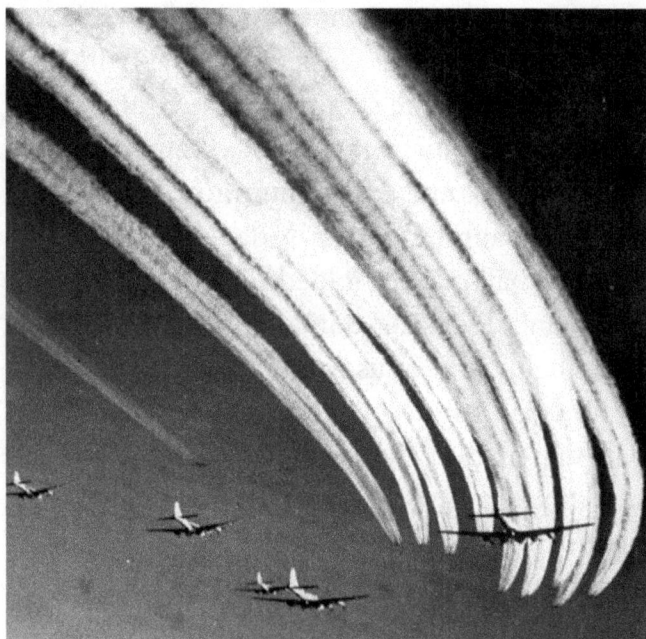

Germans know just where we were.

In one way it was inspiring to look over the whole flight and see a beautiful form in the dark sky. Sometimes, the lower group (squadron) was not in the colder atmosphere. It was dangerous for them. They knew that an attack was sure to come and they would get it first.

When a flight encountered enemy fighters, all hell would break loose. Gunners would call out incoming German planes or a B-17 that was on fire and falling out of formation. They would watch, hoping to see parachutes blossoming as the crewmembers bailed out. There were times when a B-17 would just disintegrate as fuel and bombs exploded. The noise from the gunners' firing would not distract other crewmembers because everyone was more than busy at his own battle station.

As the flight entered the target area, other incidents would take place. A plane that had caught a killing burst of flak attack might overrun another plane and seriously damage or disable it. There were several incidents were a plane was out of position during the bomb run and another plane above dropped its bombs directly on the plane below. There was no such thing as "just flying." Accidents could happen all around during a flight, and often did. Life could be extremely short.

Each mission was made up of several different groups with one of the groups as lead. We could always count on an aggressive German fighter attack as we neared the target. First there would be a single contrail from the German fighters as they formed at a higher altitude to begin their attack. Then, in small groups, down they would zoom. Each plane in our flight would watch the lead plane and when we saw it open bomb bay doors that was the signal for all planes to do the same — the IP was close.

Again, watching the lead plane when it dropped its bombs, every plane in the group would do the same. Whatever the target might be, the whole area around the target would be gone. This technique was referred to as "carpet bombing" because like a carpet, it covered everything below.

All our crews had experienced the bombings of London so we did not feel bad about the bombs we had just dropped on their city. We could not help but think about the people below who had no choice but to abide by Hitler's dictates, though.

If the plane was so shot up that its landing gear would not go down, it posed another very serious problem. All too often the plane would hit the field and skid into a ball of fire as it exploded into a mess of men and metal. Seldom did any crewmembers survive such a crash. (I was lucky; I survived my one experience.)

If the plane managed to survive a bomb run, it still had to return back to its base. Even without much battle damage it was a nerve racking return trip. Fuel was always a concern. Some of the missions were so long that if a crew did not manage the fuel correctly, they just didn't make it home. If this happened, it was enemy territory or the cold waters of the Channel.

There was no greater feeling than to see our base as we slowly took our place in the return pattern for landing. All too often, a plane would fire a red flare to announce to the ground personnel that wounded were on board and an ambulance was needed.

8TH AIR FORCE

351ST BOMB GROUP
511 BOMB SQUADRON
POLEBROOK, NORTHAMPTONSHIRE, ENGLAND

JULY 1, 1944–FEBRUARY 1, 1945

351st. Bomb Group (H)

Tail Letter: J		Missions Flown	311
Activated on: May 14, 1943		Sorties Flown	8,600
Station: Polebrook		Aircraft Lost	124
Last Mission Flown on Apr. 25 1945		# of Sorties per	
Bombs Dropped (lbs.): 20,357		A/C Missing	69.35

Special Notes: Actor Clark Gable flew with this group.

Squadrons:	508 Bomb Squadron	509 Bomb Squadron	510 Bomb Squadron	511 Bomb Squadron
Squadron Markings:	YB	RQ	TU	DS
Squadron Insignia:				

MEMBERS OF THE 511 BOMB SQUADRON

Lt. J. N. McNamara, Pilot, Compton, California; **Lt. Clyde W. Armstrong,** Co-Pilot, Texas; **Lt. Richard L. Arceneaux,** Navigator, Louisiana; **Lt. Herbert M. Miskin,** Bombardier. Long Island, New York; **T/Sgt. Carl C. Barnes,** Flight Engineer, Bakersfield, California; **T/Sgt. Eugene A. Baron,** Radio Operator, Toledo, Ohio; **S/Sgt. Gregory S. Cluett,** Ball Gunner, New York; **S/Sgt. Alfred F. Jones,** Right Waist Gunner, North Platte, Nebraska; **S/Sgt. E. J. Zourski,** Left Waist Gunner, Massachusetts; **S.Sgt. R. B. Danielson,** Tail Gunner, Nebraska; **Lt. J. N. McNamara,** Pilot, Compton, California; **Lt. Clyde W. Armstrong,** Co-Pilot, Texas; **Lt. Richard L. Arceneaux,** Navigator, Louisiana; **Lt. Herbert M. Miskin,** Bombardier, Long Island, New York; **T/Sgt. Carl C. Barnes,** Flight Engineer, Bakersfield, California; **T/Sgt. Eugene A. Baron,** Radio Operator, Toledo, Ohio; **S/Sgt. Gregory S. Cluett,** Ball Gunner, New York; **S/Sgt. Alfred F. Jones,** Right Waist Gunner, North Platte, Nebraska; **S/Sgt. E. J. Zourski,** Left Waist Gunner, Massachusetts; **S.Sgt. R. B. Danielson,** Tail Gunner, Nebraska.

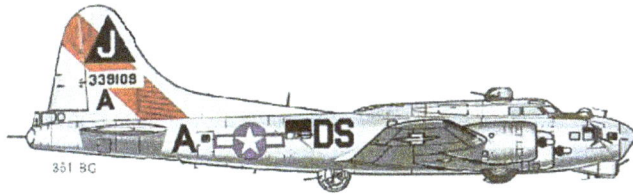

When the 351st Bomb Goup was formed, there were so few crews and planes available that each Squadron was formed into six B-17s in each squadron (see first illustration). As more crews completed training and planes were available, the individual Squadrons were changed to 4 planes in each box. Again, as more crews and more planes flew to the combat zone, they were again changed to 12 planes in each Squadron, which formed a Squadron box (see illustration, page 33). Each plane within a Squadron flew about 50 feet from te lead plane and each box then flew at a different altitude from the lead

351 st BOMB GROUP

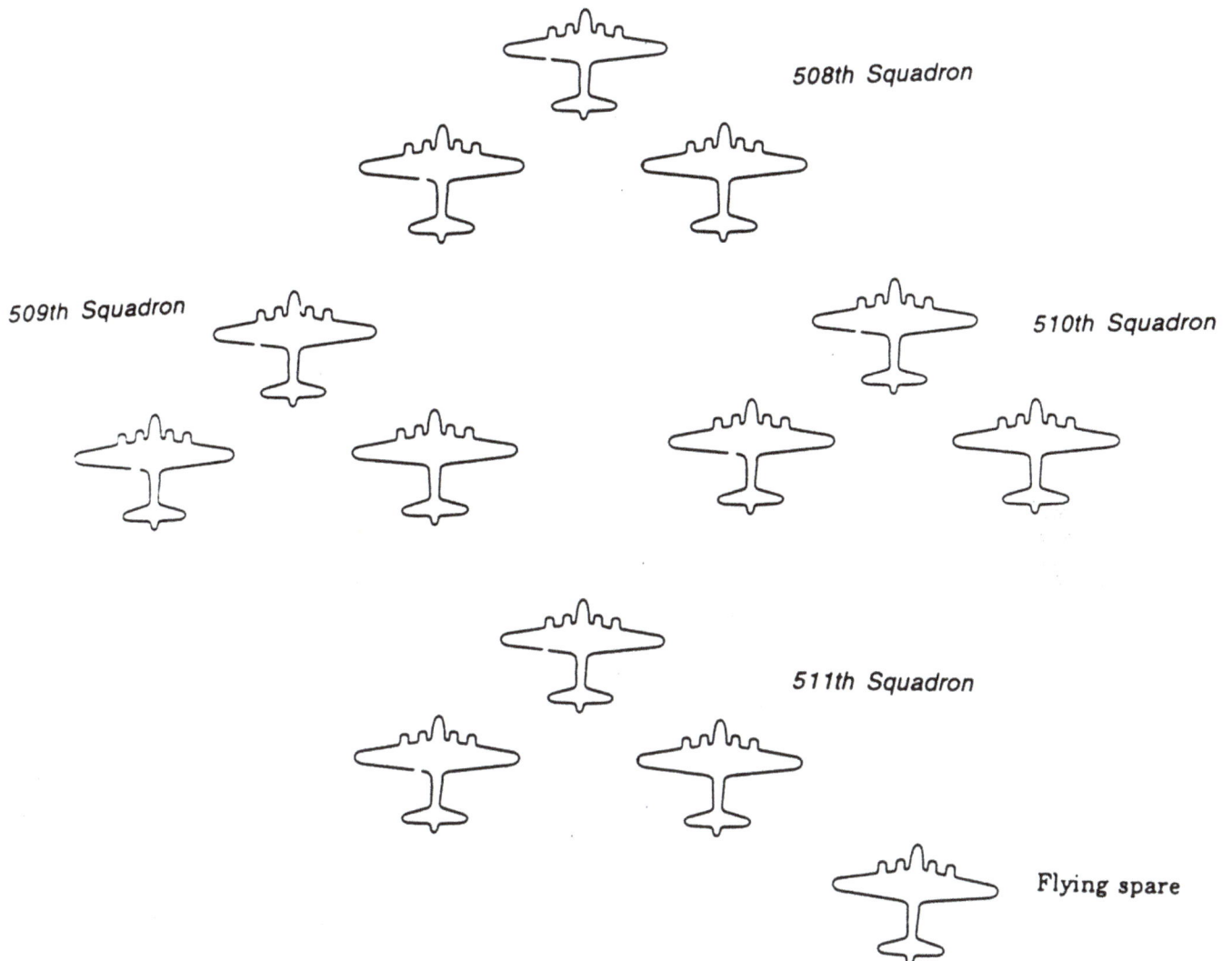

508th Squadron

509th Squadron

510th Squadron

511th Squadron

Flying spare

351 st BOMB GROUP

508th Squadron

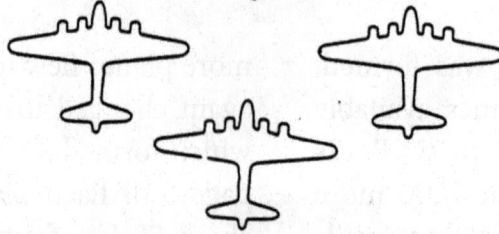

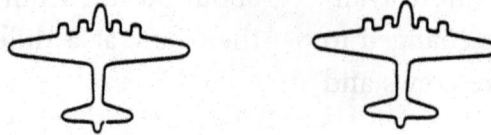

509th Squadron

510th Squadron

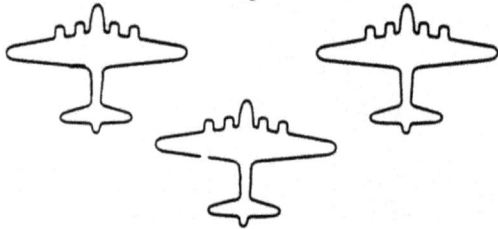

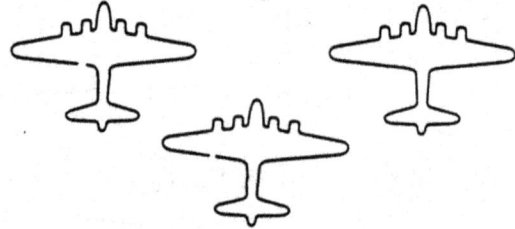

511th Squadron

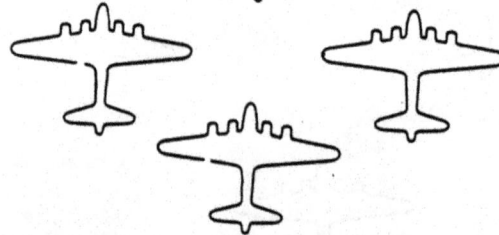

Flying spare

BASIC SPECIFICATIONS FOR B-17 MODEL G

BOEING B-17 SPECIFICATIONS

Wingspan: 103 ft. 9 in.
Length: 74 ft. 4 in.
Height: 19 ft. 1 in.
Empty Weight: 36,135 lbs
Gross Weight: 65,500 lbs
Top Speed: 287 mph
Service Ceiling: 35,600 ft.
Range: 2,000 miles w/ 6,000 lbs of bombs
Engine/Horsepower: Four Wright R-1820s/1,200 each, with General Electric turbo-superchargers
Crew: 10

Armament: Thirteen .50-in. Browning machine guns; up to 17,600 lbs of bombs The B-17G fairly bristled with defensive firepower.

- Chin, dorsal, ventral, and tail turrets each mounted a pair of guns (8).
- Left- and right-side guns in the cheeks and waist (4).
- And a single, rear-firing gun on the top of the fuselage

No wonder Luftwaffe pilots suffered from "vier motor schreck" ("four-engine fear").

The most distinctive change was the "chin" turret, sticking out below the nose. It looks like an after-thought, and it was. But the two machine guns there addressed the B-17's earlier vulnerability.

With 8,680 produced between July 1943 and April 1945, the "G" was the most numerous B-17 variant: 4,035 B-17Gs by Boeing, 2,395 by Douglas, and 2,250 by Lockheed/Vega. The vast majority of surviving B-17s are "G"s.

CREW POSITIONS IN B-17

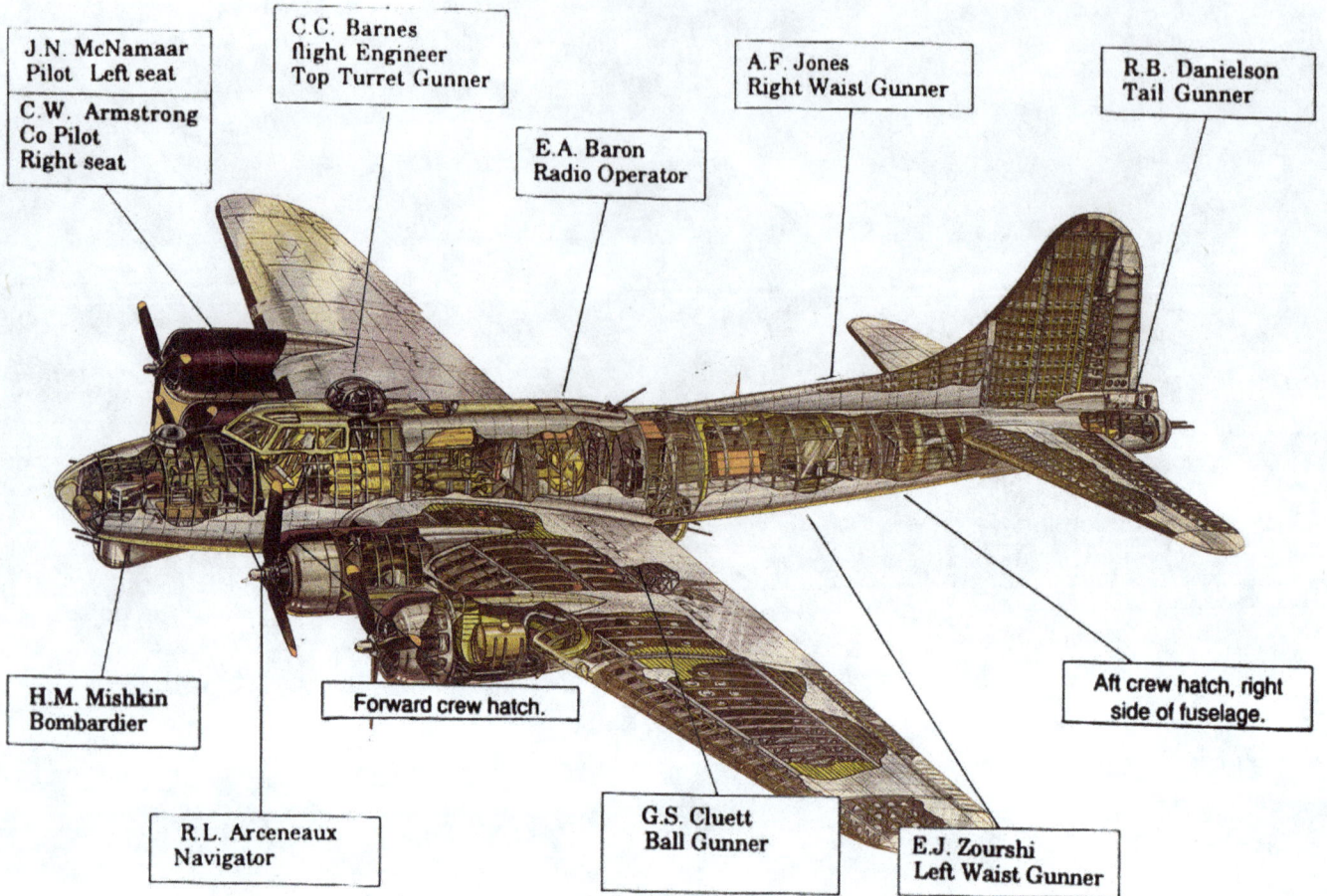

J.N. McNamaar
Pilot   Left seat

C.W. Armstrong
Co Pilot
Right seat

C.C. Barnes
Flight Engineer
Top Turret Gunner

E.A. Baron
Radio Operator

A.F. Jones
Right Waist Gunner

R.B. Danielson
Tail Gunner

H.M. Mishkin
Bombardier

Forward crew hatch.

Aft crew hatch, right
side of fuselage.

R.L. Arceneaux
Navigator

G.S. Cluett
Ball Gunner

E.J. Zourshi
Left Waist Gunner

B-17G Serial 43-338465 assigned to the 510th Bomb Squadron, 351st Bomb Group, RAF Polebrook England. This aircraft survived the war and returned to USA on 8 June 1945

RESPONSIBILITIES OF THE B-17 FLIGHT CREW

PILOT: He sits in the left cockpit flight deck position and is the commander of the aircraft. His word is law at all times and he is considered a senior highly qualified pilot with above average combat experience. He has many hours of B-17 flight experience.

CO-PILOT: His position is in the right seat of the cockpit and he is a qualified pilot but usually with little combat experience. He is in training for senior pilot. As co-pilot, he is responsible for assisting the Command Pilot in all operations of the aircraft at all times. Should the pilot become incapacitated for any reason, the co-pilot takes over command.

NAVIGATOR: His position is on the lower deck just behind the bombardier with a small navigation table. He is usually assigned the duties of "doctor" when wounded are on board. His main responsibility is to inform the pilot as to their accurate position at all times.

BOMBARDIER: He has the very best seat at all times. He sits directly in the nose of the plane and can observe everything that is forward of the flight path. His main responsibility is the bombsight. It is a highly classified aiming device that determined the accurate flight of bombs when released. The Nordon bombsight sits just in front of the bombardier and is focused through a special window. He also commands the forward 50 caliber machine guns in the nose of the Plexiglas cage. In later B-17 models, this gun became a chin turret with twin machine guns operated by a remote aiming system.

FLIGHT ENGINEER: He is responsible for the basic fitness of the plane and crew both on the

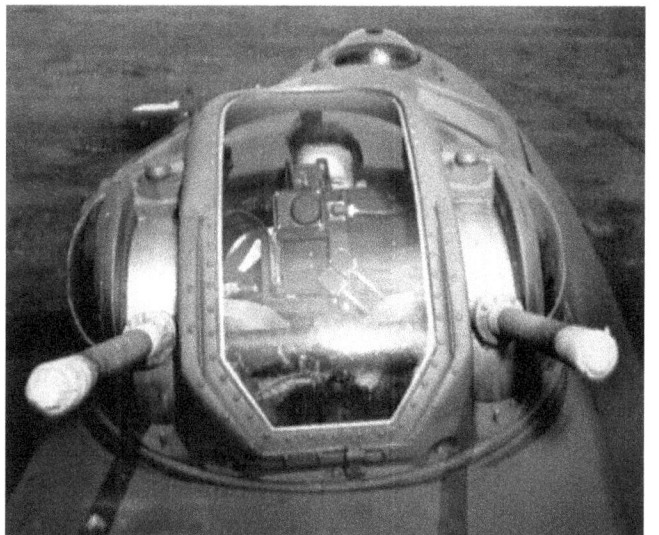

ground and in the air. His position in the air during take off and landing is just behind the two pilots. If needed, he assists in the management of the throttles and fuel mixture controls. In some cases he can fly the plane in an emergency. When the pilot asks, is the plane ready for flight?" the flight engineer had better answer with a confident "yes".

During combat his position was in the top turret with twin 50 caliber machine guns. His domain was a very restricted Plexiglas dome that was filled with a Sperry computing sight. It allowed very little room for visual observation to the outside of the plane. With the required steel helmet and his head behind the sight, the dome was completely filled. Usually Flight Engineers were qualified aircraft and machine mechanics. Prior to take off, the flight engineer took roll call and completed the crew's paperwork. This required the listing of every crewmember by serial number, rank, etc., and was handed to the ground crew chief. If the plane did not return this was the record of those killed or missing.

LEFT WAIST GUNNER: He manned a single 50-caliber machine gun pointed through a window in the center of the aircraft fuselage on the left side of the plane. He had a commanding view of everything above, below and forward of the airplane. His position was very important to the safety of the plane during an attack by enemy aircraft on the plane's left side. The Left Waist Gunner was also the assistant chief engineer.

RIGHT WAIST GUNNER: He had the same position and responsibilities as the Left Waist Gunner but covered the right side of the plane. His other responsibilities were to make sure the flack suits and maximum ammunition were on board. Each crewmember had extra assignments prior to take-off and also on their return.

RADIO OPERATOR: He had his own small area. It was on the left side of the plane and housed all of the radio communication equipment both for transmitting and receiving. In some models of the B-17, he had a single 50 caliber machine gun protruding through a small window above his position and pointing toward the back of the plane.

BALL GUNNER: The ball gunner had a world of his own. He was encased in a glassed dome hanging upside down underneath the airplane

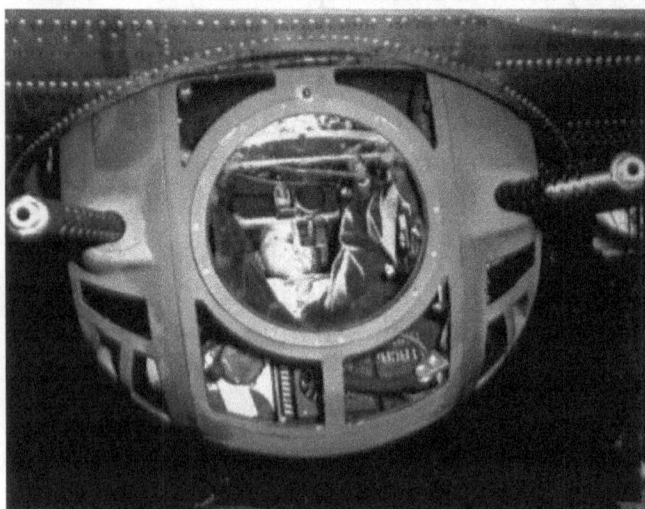

about midway of the fuselage. He manned twin 50 caliber machine guns that looked at everything that might be coming at the plane from below. This was a very cramped position that required the gunner to pull his legs up tight against his body with the operating part of the guns directly in his face. He had no room for anything but to just lay cramped up in his half-circle. He had to enter this domain through a small hatch inside the plane and required assistance to enter and exit.

TAIL GUNNER: The tail gunner had a unique position. He saw everything that had passed the flight of the plane. He was all alone in a birdcage at the very end of the plane and manned twin 50 caliber machine guns. Most enemy attacks came from the rear of the plane so this gave the tail gunner the first opportunity to inform the crew that enemy planes were about to hit their flight. He had a window on each side of his cage that allowed for limited side view, but most of

his action was directly aft. The positions listed are the normal crew responsibilities for a B-17 crew. In some cases, they may differ due to a special ability of any one of the crewmembers.

351st. Bomb Group 8th. A.F.

BOMBING RUNS

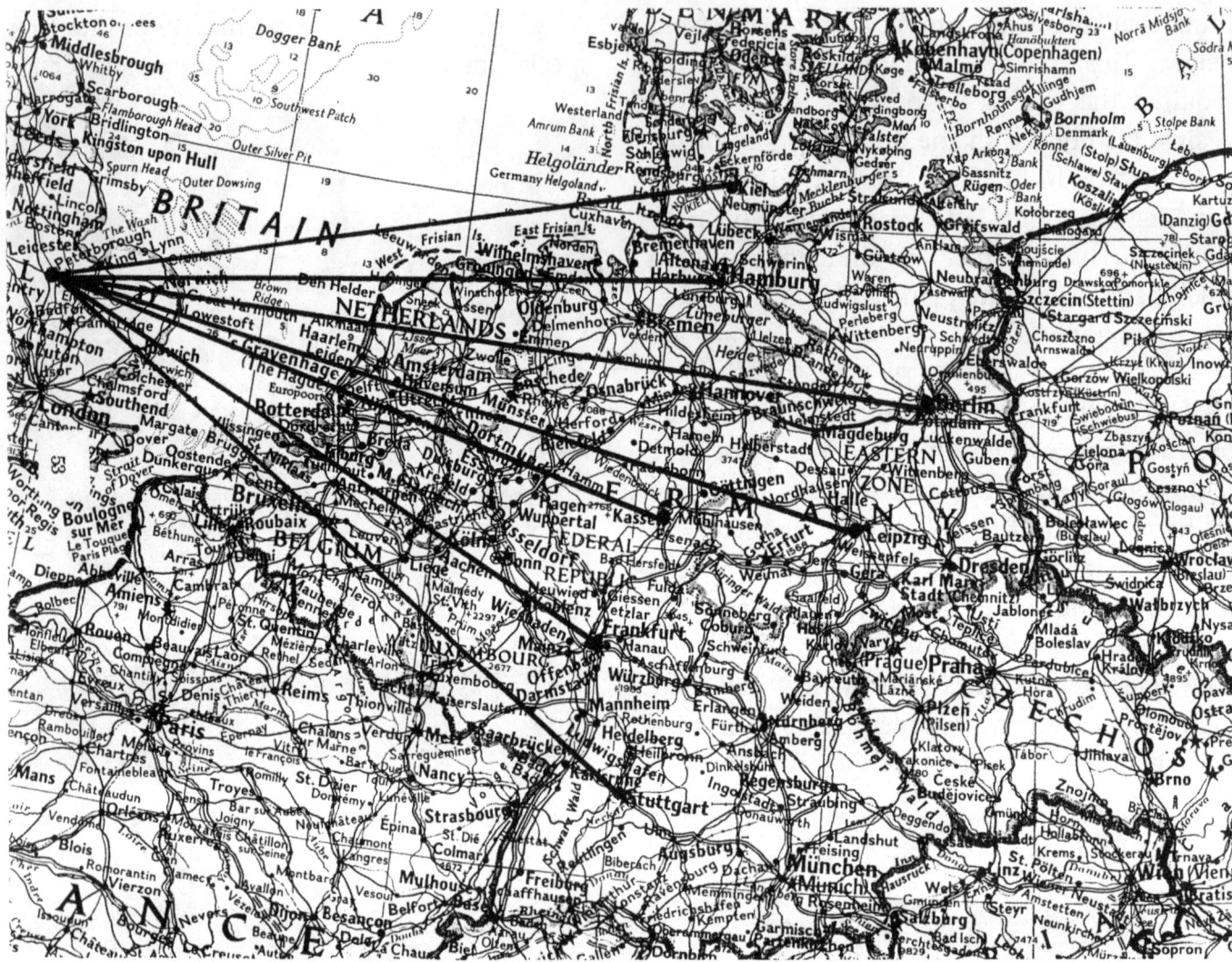

THE MISSIONS FLOWN BY CC BARNES IN CHRONOLOGICAL ORDER

MISSION #1

Berlin Germany
August 27, 1944

At our first briefing, the base commander, a colonel, had given us a glimpse of the real world. "Men, this is a real shooting war. To date, we have had about a 125% loss rate, so you can see what you and we are up against. For the pilots: if you fly as tight a formation as you can without running into the other planes in your flight, you will have the best chance of coming home. For the crew: if you consider yourself already dead and believe it and you fight as though you are dead and have nothing more to lose, then you will have a much better chance to live and also not go off the deep end due to the normal amount of fear that we all have." *(Not too long after, about mission #4 or #5, I realized just how true his statements were.)*

At 0100 hours (1 a.m.) on August 27, 1944 one of the ground staff came in our barracks yelling, telling our crew we were going to fly that day. Every one of the crew was experiencing about the same degree of first-time fear, yet we were also anxious to begin our tour of duty. I can still remember most of the emotions that I could not do much about that morning. Even though we had been briefed by the base commander and our squadron commander as to what we should expect, there was no real assurance that what they said was the way it was going to be.

Breakfast was the same old stuff, French toast with a little jelly, lots of coffee and a piece of fruit. As I tried to eat, each bite stuck deep in my throat. Even though the coffee was boiling hot, it did not seem to taste like coffee. I was too keyed up to ask myself why.

By now, the crew began to warm up to its task and a semblance of friendship became a part of our conversation. As we gathered around our newly assigned B-17, an almost new "G" model, all the training began to take over. The ground crew chief met us and directed his report to my attention. As flight engineer, I was responsible for the basic fitness of the plan and crew, both on the ground and in the air. He reported: fuel —number of gallons; ammunition — number of rounds per gun. The left engine wants to start a little slow, but it's in perfect tune. Next, he reported the bomb load and a few minor items that I should look for.

The most important item for me was a complete list of the crew — name, rank and serial number — so that if we did not return they would know exactly who went down.

We had to check out our own machine guns from the armory and make a thorough check of the weapons before we took off. It was the responsibility of each gunner to check his own weapon. Since the lives of everyone on the plane depended upon each gunner doing his job, it was extremely important.

A few minutes before scheduled "start engines," the officers arrived and gathered all of us at the front of the plane. In a clear voice, the pilot informed us of our mission for the day. I cannot express the crew's feelings as he said, "Berlin." Several weeks of hard training must have impressed the colonel since our first mission was to big Berlin. We knew Berlin was the most heavily defended city in all of Germany and that it would be one of the deadliest places to visit. I think all 10 of us felt a little sick.

For some reason, as we staged out into the early morning damp fog and cold wet of the typical English weather, the feeling of "duty, honor and country" seeped into my thoughts. I could not help but recount just why I was here and being sent out to do death to someone who wanted to do the same to me. Someone whom I had never seen. What a crazy world we were living in.

We were assigned the spare slot and felt pretty good about our chances of not having to go to Berlin on our first mission. We were the last to take off and would fly along side the formation as far as the enemy coast. If any of the regular mission planes should have to drop out, the spare (us) takes its place and flies the mission.

Engines started, we taxied out to our assigned position for take off and again learned that we had the distinction of being the vice lead. What had we done, not having flown even one mission, to be assigned such an honor? We were second in command of the squadron mission!

Even in the early morning mist, our take off was near perfect and we climbed out of the over-

cast into the beginning of the day. Little did we know what kind of day we would have.

Everyone on our plane was praying that no one would have to drop out. Berlin was not the place for first-timers. I was watching the lead box, as the right wing man wasn't holding his position very well. All at once, he dropped out and headed back to our base. Our hearts sank.

We pulled into his place and got as close to the lead plane as we could. We said to the pilot, "Mac keep us in as good a position in the formation as you can, and we will take care of the Germans." I don't know how the lead plane felt about having a green crew on his wing. Other experienced crews had said, "The German can tell a green crew and really go after them." It made us feel that we were dead on our first mission and that is why we fought so hard to stay alive.

As the crew settled down and began to check each position's readiness for combat, the pilot began his routine. First, radio check for all crew. Next, we heard the pilot ask the navigator to put the plane on its assigned course to join the group and then go on into enemy territory. The tension began to rise.

From the very first day back in Ardmore, Oklahoma, when we first formed our crew, our training was strict and targeted for just such a day. Now the training took over. Each item was checked and rechecked. The only items we did not have in the states were flak jackets. We made sure that they were in place and they gave a small measure of security — but just a little.

Next was the command to put on our oxygen masks. Our flight to Berlin would take us north, just off the coast of Norway, then down in a southern course into Germany and to our target. Each crewmember was wearing heavy, high-altitude clothing and even with the temperature at about 50 degrees below zero, sweat began to fill our suits.

Somewhere before we began our turn for the final leg, the group lead plane had to drop out. This is where we received some notoriety. Now we were the lead for our squadron and all of the remaining planes in our squadron would fly off of our course and control. They would bomb when we dropped our bombs and pray as we were praying.

As the total bomb groups began the turn on our final leg to the target, the German fighters showed up — Messerschmitt 109s and Fockewulfs by the dozen. They were tiny, black, fast-moving specks far off to the left of the formation, flying back to our end groups. They would fly far out of our firing range, then, at a much higher altitude from our flight, swing along in the same direction we were going but again out of range. Every gun of our flight tracked the fast-moving enemy planes as they moved to the front of our formation. Our average ground speed was about 200 mph, while the German fighters could attain speed of nearly 400 mph.

As they reached ahead of our flight, they would look for any B–17s that might be a little out of position and an easy target. The easy target would then get all the fighters' attention and, in most instances, receive serious damage if not be shot out of the formation.

At the same time, many of the fighters would attack the whole bomb group head on, screaming through at their highest speed. There would be, at best, two seconds for us to fire at them. As top turret gunner, I would begin my tracking of the fighters when they were out of range. When my Sperry automatic lead sight filled to the right range, I let go with all I had. After the first pass, I remember that my flight suit seemed full of

sweat, even though we were still flying at 26,000 feet in 50 degree below zero temperatures.

The fight was many air miles from our target, yet we were getting the hell shot out of the group. Off to the right, there was a flash and one of the B-17s in another squadron exploded and fell to the ground in many pieces. Ten very brave young men had just ceased to exist. I could not help the painful, empty feeling in my stomach. For the first time, I knew how close to death we were … just seconds.

As we came onto our IP and the target for the first time, the heavy black bursts of flak filled the sky at just the correct altitude to tear our formation apart. It was like a carpet across the sky. Soon, several of the planes began to stream smoke from one or more engines as we began our bomb run.

The pilot asked our bombardier, "Are you on target?"

With an affirmative response, the bombardier took over control of the plane. "Bombay doors open, standby, bombs away." The plane took a sharp jump in altitude as 6,000 pounds of high explosives left it.

Next was a sharp turn to vacate the target area and set the course for our return flight to England. The only crewmember that could see the results of our bomb run was the tail gunner, R. B. Danielson. He reported that the entire target area was one big cloud of smoke and fire. I guess we did okay for a first mission.

The German fighters were just as determined to keep us from going home, as we were to get there. As we'd approached the target, the fighters had been like angry hornets attacking the formation with great determination. Now that we had rained death and great damage down on their most important city, they were really mad.

The fighters came in much closer and fired with more skill than they had earlier. There was not time for any thought of fear. Each of the crew knew his job by rote and executed it with precision.

It sent a cold cheer through the plane when the right waist gunner shouted that he had exploded one of the Messerschmitt 109s. There was no time to cheer; there were far too many others bent on shooting us down.

There were reports of the German fighters' 20mm shells passing thru the plane from different positions of the crew. There was a shudder through the plane as we took a direct hit in our number four engine and fire blossomed from the wing.

I looked out at the engine and my heart took a completely new leap. As flight engineer, I knew that the burning engine meant real trouble. Instantly, the pilot released the fire extinguisher, and thankfully, the fire went out. If the fuel tank in that wing had been ruptured and the spilling fuel had reached the red-hot supercharger, we would have been one big ball of flame and smoke. Thank God for great favors.

There were several different groups in our total formation and as we hastily vacated Berlin, I could see several more B-17s losing altitude as they dropped out of the formation and headed for German soil. More prisoners of war, or worse. (The United States Government regrets to inform you that…)

The English Channel glistened far out in front of us. We were clearing the enemy air space and the fear slowly left us. As I looked down at the base of my top turret, the deck was littered with spent 50 caliber rounds. I guessed that I had fired over 500 rounds.

During training in the states, when I fired the guns, I was well aware of the blasting noise. Twin 50s make one heck of a lot of noise when your head is tucked between the two guns. During the air battle that had just passed, I was not aware of the guns making any noise. It seemed impossible.

As we left the main land of Europe and headed back over the North Sea, each of the crew took a deep, clean breath of air. So far; so good. We had survived our first mission — only 24 more to go. *(At the time we became active in England, 25 missions was all each crew had to do. At about our 18th mission, the number was extended to 35 missions.)*

Several badly shot-up planes had wounded on board. As they entered the landing pattern, a red flare was fired from the aircraft to alert the ground personnel that there were wounded on board so that medical people would stand by.

After we were at our hard stand and began to deplane, we could see some of the wounded being removed and noted that several of the crewmen were carried out completely covered by a blanket. This had been their final flight. Rest with God.

Landing back at our base did not allow for any respite. First, all the gunners had to take their machine guns to the armory and I had to go over the plane with the ground chief engineer. We counted all the holes and the damage to our number-four engine.

Next was a debriefing where each crewmember was asked a never-ending bunch of questions about the mission. "Did you…? How many fighters? Where did they come from? What color were their markings" … and on and on until the interrogators were satisfied that they had a picture of the mission. It was amazing that there were so many different images of the battle from each crewmember.

No one was more surprised than our crew that we made our first mission over Berlin and returned alive. I think that the crew chief, after he learned of our mission target, felt that sending a green crew to Berlin, he had better order another plane. After that we always had a good place in the formation and never had to fly "tail end Charley." We flew a good first mission and were very grateful to get back to the base. *(One item, if the spare turns back because no other plane has to abort, the spare does not receive credit for a mission. Generally if you start flying tail end Charlie, you don't have much chance of getting credit.)*

As I went to the barracks to get rid of my flight gear, I went over most of what the crewmembers had said about the raid and shuddered. I asked myself, *Really? Did all that happen? We could have been killed.*

I had some post flight paperwork that had to be done by the next morning. After I completed what I thought was correct, I joined some of the 511 crews. We paddled our bicycles to a pub about a mile down a dirt road from our base. As most of us relived the first mission, we thought that God must have had better plans for the ten men of our crew.

Each of the following missions, #2 through #35, were about the same depending upon the target assigned to us. There were no "milk runs" as far as I was concerned. For every mission there were at least two planes that were shot down and never came home. As noted in the individual worst missions, some were far more dreadful than others.

MISSION #2
PEENEMUNDE, GERMANY
August 30, 1944

This mission came about through the capture of a German general in France. He had papers showing he had been in Pennemunde. The base was thought to be an R&R (rest) base. The General denied that he had ever been on

R&R so the British flew a reconnaissance flight over the base. The photos showed it was a testing facility for V-1 and V-2 rocket bombs. The photos showed a lot of large high-pressure tanks and test stands.

It was an early breakfast, then to the briefing to learn what the day would bring. Our crew always sat in the front of the briefing room so that we could see how much string was hanging below the mission curtain. It was one way to tell how long the mission was going to be. There was no string hanging below the curtain, so we knew it would be another long day.

We had a normal takeoff and joined our formation. Peenemunde is on the north coast of Germany on the Baltic Sea, east of Kiel. We were flying at 27,000 feet and flew south of our target. We then made a 180-degree turn so that we would have the wind at our back.

I saw the fighters coming at us from the north and over the water. First, it was the deadly flak and it was bad. The fighters were determined to shoot us down. Our bomb release was right on target. The rocket fuel made one gigantic explosion and fire.

This mission cost the Germans six months in lost development time on their rocket program.

MISSION #3

Kiel, Germany
September 9, 1944

This was the third time I thought I would not get back to England. Kiel lay in the furthermost part of Germany, just off the coast from Denmark. Flying time to target was about six hours and 30 minutes. That was a long way to have to fight off massive attacks by the dreaded Luftwaffe — the German Air Force.

Our target was a massive warehouse installation that stored vast supplies and war material that was shipped down from Norway and other German-occupied countries, and then shipped on to the ground forces of the German armies.

As we came within fighter range near the coast of the Netherlands, the battle began. Flight after flight of Messerschmitt 109s attacked from high above, diving through our formation. On each side of our group, I could see one B-17 after another being hit hard and set on fire or just going down.

As we approached our IP, the bombardier called out the targets and soon we felt the upward lift as bombs left the plane and headed for the targets. Our flight really blew the whole installation to pieces.

As we departed the target area, flak enclosed our plane and soon we had only one working engine. We dropped from 27,000 feet to about 18,000 feet in an almost vertical dive. I thought we were going on in … this was it.

Messershmitt BE 109

Finally at 18,000 feet, the pilot brought the plane under control and headed straight for the open sea and the English Channel. You can't fly very far with only one engine set at full throttle, but if the pilot is skilled the plane can glide for a great distance.

We set a two-degree glide and watched as we gradually descended toward the sea. We went into the cold water some 12 miles off Holland and 60 miles from England. Before we hit water, everyone got into the radio room except the pilot. As soon as the plane hit the water, it began to sink. We popped the dingy, released the hatch at the top of the radio room and jumped into the floating dinghies.

Quickly we loaded the emergency equipment and cast off as the B-17 slid into the depths of the cold North Sea. We tied the two dinghies together and set up our radio antenna, the "Gibson Girl" — a hand cranked radio transmitter. We then inflated the balloon that carried the antenna aloft. With the Gibson Girl, you hand crank and it automatically sends out a special SOS radio signal so that a rescue boat can find the downed crew.

We had been in the cold water for several hours by 9 p.m. (2100 hours) and it was dark. We were ready to give up. After a long, miserable and cold wait, we saw a light sweeping the surface of the water and headed our way.

We jumped up in our dinghies and shouted, "They're coming to get us! They're here! They're here! The Britts are coming!"

The waist gunner shouted, "What if they're Germans?"

We were only about 12 miles off the coast of German-held territory and 60 miles from England. We realized it *could* be Germans and suddenly we were scared and our hearts dropped to the bottom of our shoes. Finally they picked us up in the spotlight and the boat pulled up alongside. We froze. We weren't sure if we would be machine-gunned or rescued.

At last, one of the rescuing seamen shouted, "I say there, ole chap. Sir, are you all right?" I will tell you, we were all right then.

We jumped up and the Britts pulled us onto their boat and gave us some very welcome hot tea and sandwiches. *(The Britts can find tea at the best of times.)* It was really great after being in the cold sea for hours.

The rescuers machine-gunned our dinghies, sinking them, and then took us back to England so we could continue to fly our missions and fight the Germans.

MISSION #4
Ludwigshaven, Germany
September 10, 1944

The 508th was lead squadron for this mission. Ludwigshaven is across the Rhine River from Mannheim in southern Germany. We flew across Belgium and northeast France, approaching the target from the southwest to again have a strong tail wind that would increase our speed. It was the best way to get over the target as fast as we could and clear the flak zone. There was plenty of black death, anyway.

MISSION #5
Dulmen, Germany
September 12, 1944

The primary briefed target was Wessel, Germany, but heavy cloud cover was so high that we were directed to our secondary target, Dulmen. The target area was a big fuel dump.

Dulmen is about 30 miles southwest of Munster. Flying time was 8 hours and 30 minutes. This day, the Germans used up a lot of flak ammunition.

Our whole crew felt that we would not return to our base that night when we took off that morning. The score was, "who would get back and who wouldn't." This was the fourth time I thought the end was near, but somehow God let me live.

Flying to the target was no different than any of the other difficult missions. The German fighters met us at the usual point and swept down through the flight, firing cannons and machine guns at their choice of targets. There were Messerschmitt 109s, and Fockewulfs fighter planes. Their pilots were really good. They would pick out a B-17 and keep firing at it until it was on fire or just exploded.

As we approached our target, the flak was like black clouds bursting at different altitudes in all direction. Burst after burst tried to feel out our aircraft. As I looked back at the trailing squadron, the triangle "C" flak all but blotted out the sky around and behind them. It was impossible to think that we had just flown through that same flak and so far had not been hit.

MISSION #6
Merseburg, Germany
September 17, 1944

Our target was one of the main oil refineries. Flying time was 8 hours and 30 minutes, making for a long day. Merseberg is deep inside Germany, just west of Leipzig.

Our route took us over Belgium and France, across the Rhine and south of Koblenz. We were far enough north of Frankfort to be out of the range of the heavy flak guns and northeast of our target. This was the first time that the Germans sent up JU-88 bombers against us. They lobed rockets at our formation and that exploded in the midst of the formation.

This was really scary. One rocket went off just under our tail and blew out the tire on our tail wheel, but we didn't know it until we got back to our base.

MISSION #7
Munster, Germany
September 19, 1944

The target at Munster was vast rail marshaling yard. It was a short flight of 5 hours and 30 minutes.

Munster put up the heaviest flak that we had yet encountered at any target. One great burst, just in front of our nose, felt like it had stopped the plane dead in the air. Our fuselage and wings were full of holes from that one burst.

MISSION #8
Frankfort, Germany
September 25, 1944

The Messerschmitt 109s had been a constant threat to our missions and now we could get even. Our target at Frankfort was a large ME-109 engine factory and we were extremely pleased to blow it to hell.

Our squadron, the "511," was the lead squadron. It was a nice clear day and we could see the Rhine River with the factory on the north side of the river, east of the town. Our route was across France, cross the Rhine at Koblenz, then due east to Frankfort.

As usual the flak was impressive. With over 400 flak batteries, they could put up a deadly black cloud at our bombing altitude that was totally intimidating. We were bounced around a good bit on the bomb run.

The group lost some planes, but we were again lucky and made it back to our base.

MISSION #9
Eschweiler, Germany
September 26, 1944

The target was another important railroad yard. Destroy the rail yards and the Germans

can't get supplies to the group troops at their front lines.

Again, our bomb load was right on target. This mission was only 5 hours.

MISSION #10
Cologne, Germany
September 27, 1944

Our target was another railroad yard. Cologne was one of the main centers for rail distribution for all traffic going west out of Germany. It supplied everything to the troops.

We had plenty of heavy flak over the target. Flight time 5 hours and 40 minutes.

MISSION #11
Kassel, Germany
October 2, 1944

Our route was a rare circular one taking us in over the Zuider Zee in Holland and back out south of Koblenz. It turned out to be pretty hair-raising because we lost one engine shortly after crossing into Holland.

We did not want to turn back at that point, so we crunched down in our stations and flew on with the hope that we could stay with the flight. We were not able to do so and slowly drifted back from one group to another in the long bomber stream. We dropped our bomb load on Kassel with the last group.

When we turned toward home, we were all by ourselves. The pilot put the plane down on the deck to get under the clouds and, by the grace of God, we made it back.

MISSION #12
Sterkrade, Germany
October 3, 1944

We had bombed oil refineries before, but this was a new one — a synthetic oil plant. Stekrade is in the north end of the Ruhr Valley.

Concentrated flak batteries heavily defended the whole valley and the absence of clouds allowed the guns to be extremely accurate. I saw more planes shot down on this mission than on any other mission. We had heavy contrails at the bombing altitude, so there was no way we could hide.

MISSION #13
Plauen, Germany
October 5, 1944

The target at Plauen was another different target. There were several large chemical and explosives factories in the area. Plauen is near the Czechoslovakian border and it was a very long mission.

German 262 jets were in the target area and they would make high speed passes through the formation trying to disable one of the B-17s, making it easier for the Messerschmitt 109s to have a field day.

It was a 9 hour and 45 minute flight and we were really beat by the time we got back to home base.

MISSION #14
Stettin, Germany
October 7, 1944

Our mission to Stettin began much like our previous missions, with a lousy, dark wake-up call, then staggering in the dark for heavy high altitude clothing. Once dressed, we went out to eat a breakfast of stacks of cold French toast, coffee and, maybe, some orange marmalade.

As the breakfast ended, the crews would gather and grope their way to the briefing room to finally learn just where the day was to take us. We would groan as the briefing officer called out the mission. Next would be checking out any special cold weather gear and, of course, getting a parachute and, sometimes, a big thermos of coffee.

At the plane, each flight crewmember would go over his station knowing that the ground crew had already done so many times during their routine pre-flight checks. It was our butts on the line, and we just wanted to have that extra measure of sureness that each man had the right stuff for the day.

As each crewman checked in with the pilot, I would begin the engine start and run up checks, making sure that each of the four engines were going to give maximum power for takeoff and the long flight to the target. As we began our roll for mission number 14, all the different problems that had occurred on the previous missions quickly counted down in my mind. Just another "make sure" check.

The briefing officer informed the group that the mission for the day was "Stettin" — a place that none of us had heard of before. Now, here we were, rolling down the darkened runway headed out to blow it off the map.

According to our maps, Stettin was north of the city of Berlin, the place we bombed on our first mission. Stettin was on the Neisse River that intersects with the Baltic Sea and the border of Germany and Poland. This was going to be another long flight and the target was another highly defended oil refinery.

On our approach to the target, the Germans must have thought our target was Berlin. The Messerschmitt 109s and Fockewulfs came at us like mad hornets and gave us a devastating work over before we even got close to our target.

For this mission, we had a new ball gunner who had joined us from the Army infantry. He said, "You fly boys have a much better deal than us guys on the ground. You come back to a hot meal, sleep in barracks with clean sheets, and have a place to lean back and rest and enjoy yourselves." So, that is what he wanted ... a piece of the good life while fighting the war.

As we entered the enemy's air space, he folded himself down into the ball turret and realized that his battle station was a little cramped. Just before we got to our IP, he saw flak bursting through the clouds at the flight just ahead of us. The infantry guy commented, "Boy, those guys are really getting the hell shot out of them." He was told that we were headed the same way to get to our target and we had to go through the same flak. We never heard another word from him. He put his flak jacket over the window.

As we came to the target, the sky was full of the deadly black bursts exploding all around us.

One of the bursts took out our number-3 engine and another burst exploded just above my top turret, knocking me out of the turret and down to the plane's floor.

A piece of flak had passed through my Plexiglas dome and hit the right side of my head. The blow knocked me out and I fell on the floor behind the pilot. When I came to, we were in a steep dive.

The pilot got the plane under control at about 10,000 feet. With the number-3 engine smoking badly, we took a course out over the Baltic Sea and headed west. Twelve planes out of our formation were so badly shot up that they staggered into Sweden to be interned for the duration of the war in order to save the crews.

It took some great flying to get us back to the base. When all had settled down, the bombardier began the routine oxygen check. He couldn't get any response from the ball turret gunner so he asked the waist gunner to check on him.

The waist gunner cranked the turret up into the plane and opened the hatch. The ball gunner was so frightened that he couldn't even speak. They got him out and sat him down in the radio room and covered him with blankets. That was the only flight he ever went on and he could not get back into the infantry fast enough. He said, "In the infantry, at least you can dig a hole."

As we flew back toward England, we were just a few feet above the Baltic Sea. The navigator carefully plotted our course across the Netherlands to miss the areas where we could encounter more German fighters and heavy flak. I kept transferring fuel to the good engines to make sure that we had enough fuel to make it back to our field.

We had been reported missing in action, so we had to go to supply to get our stuff back. At debriefing, I wanted to keep my steel helmet to show the big crease in the side, but I didn't get to. The officer responsible for receiving new crews wanted to keep it to show how important it was to wear all of the flak gear. He said that if I had not had it on, I surely would have been killed.

The moment that our plane returned from the mission, the ground crew began a detailed inspection of the plane, checking every item and making any repairs that might be needed. On most occasions, holes in

An example of a German 12.8cm FlaK anti-aircraft artillery system.

the plane would have to be repaired by over-worked sheet metal specialists and then all control surfaces would be tested.

The engines would be carefully evaluated. If they were due for special time checks, the mechanics took care of that function. Usually spark plugs would need replaced There was always a shortage of plugs, so the ground crew would have to re-manufacture the old ones by careful cleaning and re-setting the plug spark gap.

Then there were the tires, the bomb racks, and hydraulic systems, even cleaning up some poor crewman's position where he may have had to toss his French toast during the earlier flight. The flight crew depended upon the ground crew for the basic operation of all aspects of the plane. It fell to me to make sure that they did their jobs carefully and correctly. This was just routine every day and night.

Again, the end of one bad day and a frightening mission. Just 21 more to go!

MISSION #15
Cologne, Germany
October 14, 1944

This would be our second trip to Cologne. We still remembered the heavy flak that greeted us on our 10th mission. The same railroad yard was there, but had undergone major repairs. It was the main route for shipping supplies to all the German troops on the western front. We could bomb it out today and they would have the trains running tomorrow.

Flying time 5 hours and 45 minutes.

MISSION #16
Rhuland, Germany
October 15, 1944

We knew the morning we took off that some of us would not return to our base. This was the fourth time I felt I would not get back, but again, God lent a hand and allowed me to go on.

The flight to the target involved one attack after another. The fighters came in droves and the few seconds that we could fire on them seemed like an annoyance to them.

Our bombardier had just let our bombs go, right on target, when a heavy burst of flak exploded just in front of our number-2 engine, knocking it out.

My combat station was the top turret gunner. As the flak blew the number-2 engine, I felt something hit me in the left side of my chest, just over my heart.

At first, I thought maybe I was dead. After a few seconds, I was able to get my breath back and I realized that I was still breathing and not dead. I then thought that I might have lost my left arm and shoulder. In the top turret I could only see up and through the gun sight, there was just barely room for my head.

I finally got enough courage to try to move my fingers. They moved. I tried my arm, it moved without pain. I got down out of the turret to see just what had happened. The chest parachute straps were folded about ten times over my chest so they were about an inch thick. A piece of flak had pierced the plane, cut through my parachute harness, ripped my flight suit under my arm and lodged in the bomb bay door.

We could not wear our parachutes while at our battle stations because there was not enough room. There were two locking hooks on the front of the harness that held the chute to one's body. My harness was now useless. I was in deep trouble should the plane be hit hard. If I'd had to jump, as soon as the parachute opened I would just keep going down. I was really scared all the way back to England.

I was so concerned that I might be dead, and so relieved I wasn't, that I was unaware I had also been hit in the leg, just below the knee. My electrical suit was shorted and at the altitude we were flying the temperature is well below zero. My feet froze on our return and I still carry a piece of the flak in my left leg. It bothers me to this day when I get too cold.

MISSION #17

Cologne, Germany
October 17, 1944

It seems as though we cannot blow that darned railroad system to hell. This mission was just like the other two. We lost more planes.

MISSION #18

Hanover, Germany
October 24, 1944

Each new mission seems to be tougher and more dangerous. The crew still had the really bad feelings leftover from mission #14 buried deep in our thoughts. We had been to Cologne on the 17th mission and that made our 5th trip to that target. I began to wonder just how many trips it would take to wipe out a good sized German city.

The 8th Air Force had been at the daylight bombing method for about 2-1/2 years, and still the Germans were able to put up a large number of fighters and always had blankets of flak to greet each mission that we flew. Maybe this one to Hanover today would be different.

My nerves were past the breaking point and the only way I could force myself to get back into the B-17 again was the honor of being part of a great crew — that, and none of us wanted to let the others down. I simply shuddered, told myself God would give me the right to live through just one more mission and then I could rest for awhile.

(At the end of each mission, I hugged the ground, swore that I would not go another time and kissed the ground.)

At the next mission, each crewmember would be geared up at his station and ready for whatever the mission might bring. Most of us had written ourselves off for returning home, so with an "already dead" attitude, we could mask our true feelings. We just did what we were trained to do — climbed on board, took our positions and flew into the hell that we were sure to meet.

Back to October 22, 1944 and the mission to Hanover. It wasn't a bad weather day. Broken, big puffy clouds scattered across the flight path made us feel a little better. If we could mask our flight in the clouds, maybe the German fighters would not see us.

At 15,000 feet we went on oxygen and began the testing of the 50-caliber machine guns. Each station checking in said, "Okay."

The German ground gunners who fired the high altitude flak must have gone back to school because as we approached our target, the bursts were extremely accurate and the Messerschmitt 109s were even more persistent.

As we entered the target area, several mean and deadly bursts of flak took out two of our engines. We dropped out of formation, leaving an ominous dark trail of smoke. The number-four engine was on fire and it seemed that every German fighter was on us for the final kill.

With the pilot barely controlling the plane, we dove for the clouds to avoid the fighters that were zeroing in on us. It seemed like several forevers before the clouds hid us and gave us a measure of false safety and some breathing time. Again, flying as low as we could, we made for the English Channel, while hiding as best we could in the clouds.

With only the two engines to keep us airborne, our speed was ploddingly slow. Hiding in the clouds was rough but no German fighters found us. We kind of chugged along over the Channel's cold waters and looked down at the white caps.

Remembering an earlier mission when we had to ditch in the channel caused a cold shiver to run down my back. It seemed funny, being worried about cold water when coming off a deadly near-destroyed mission.

The time it took to fly over the 40 miles of Channel on just two engines made us over an hour late getting back to the base. The base personnel assumed that we had been shot down and some of our flight had already returned reporting us down.

The supply staff had gathered our personal effects, bedding and such, and stored them for final disposition. (When you were missing in action your belongings were picked up and stored. In time your personal belongings would be sent home and the government items were sent to Supply.) So, we had to go to supply and retrieve all of our gear, make-up the beds again, go to interrogation, eat and cleanup.

I was supposed to meet a girlfriend at a nearby pub. The pubs were our meeting place after returning from a mission so we could figure out who had not returned. The public places had to have blackout curtains over all doors and windows.

Some of the returning crews had told my girl that I had been shot down. We gave each other a big hug; everyone in the pub was watching. Then I had to tell everyone in the pub how we had evaded the Jerries and returned on just two engines.

At that time in the air war, it was an everyday way of life or death. One never knew if he would be back. A girl might be your girl one day and another guy's girl tomorrow. When so many crews failed to return from each mission, I could not help but think, *Would I be next?*

MISSION #19
Hamburg, Germany
October 25, 1944

The orders were to blow up another major oil refinery. The route would take us over the North Sea, turning into shore opposite the city of Hamburg with the returning route the same way. The tail gunner reported that our bombs really caused a lot of damage with massive fires everywhere. As usual when attacking an oil refinery, the flak was unusually heavy.

Our flight time was 6 hours and 30 minutes.

MISSION #20
Gelsenkirchen, Germany
October 26, 1944

Coke was an important product for Germany, since it was needed in order to produce steel. Gelsenkirchen was a large coke plant at the northern end of the Ruhr Valley. Several of our earlier missions had taken us through the valley and, as usual, there was deadly flak.

It was our time to fly lead. The 511 were making the Germans feel some real pain.

Flying time 5 hours and 50 minutes.

MISSION #21
Munster, Germany
October 30, 1944

Munster also had large marshaling yards. Heavy flak greeted us going in and there was more as we departed the target area. The weather was really bad, but we persisted and did all we could to keep supplies from reaching the German field troops.

Flying time: 6 flying hours.

MISSION #22
Berlin, Germany
November 16, 1944

There is one special mission that stands out forever in my mind. The 22nd mission was our second time to the dreaded big "B" — Berlin. Germany's capitol city lay in near rubble. Regardless, they defended it with the tenacity of a devil.

The routine started as usual, wake up at 0100 hours (1 a.m.) and stagger around trying to recover from loss of sleep caused by our last mission. Somehow, my clothes refused to fit. They just didn't want to go over my tired body. Finally shaking around just enough so that I felt reasonably comfortable, I, along with the rest of our crew, sloshed through the ever-present mud to the mess hall and breakfast.

As we looked up into the darkness of the morning, fog held right down to the ground. My first thought was, *Maybe we will get cancelled and I can go back to the cold barracks and get some more sleep.* Sleep was a precious item that war did not allow.

When I'd finished breakfast, it was my responsibility to make sure all the crew carefully checked their guns and high altitude flight gear. The flight gear was designed to electrically heat the body when were flying above 15,000 feet in altitude. At that height and above the temperature was always below zero. The higher we flew, the colder it became, sometimes as low as 50 or more degrees below the zero mark. Frostbite was a common problem.

The pilot, copilot, navigator and bombardier attended the briefing right after breakfast. We could usually guess the target for the day by the sounds coming from the briefing room. This morning a loud moan was emitted as the briefing officer raised the curtain covering the map of the flight plan and the target.

Hearing this, most of the crew just dropped their heads and went on getting the plane ready. When the pilot arrived, he wanted the plane in full readiness without any excuses. If it wasn't, I received the brunt of his dissatisfaction.

The front office crew slowly made their way to the parked aircraft and it was obvious they were just as unhappy as we were. Nonetheless, the pilot announced that the target for the morning mission was Berlin. We would have some 8 to 10 hours of flight time.

I knew we would be meeting several hundred of Germany's best fighter pilots on this flight and some of us would not be coming back. On such a long flight over the worst of the enemy homeland, we would be fighting strong attacks just as soon as we entered the Germany's borders and would have to fight all the way back. The German fighters had a real advantage over our mission. Going in, fighters would attack as fiercely as they could … usually until they ran out of fuel and ammunition. They would land and refuel and re-arm and wait for our return, when they would hit us again.

To make sure we would return as best I could, I worked out a deal with the Armament Sergeant at the base for as much extra ammunition as we dared take. (It was very much against policy to carry extra ammunition.) Each additional pound of weight caused us to use that much more fuel, and on a long flight we needed all the fuel we could store. Sometimes we wished we had more.

McMamarr gathered the crew around and tried to assure each of us that if we all did our usual great jobs, we would go to Berlin and return. Most of us were not that sure.

About this time, the crew looked at the fog and, just as I had, said a little prayer that our mission would be cancelled. As it turned out, no such luck.

Sunrise was supposed to be minutes before 08:00, so take off was scheduled for 06:45 so it would be in the dark. As the pilot climbed into our B-17, he asked as he always did, "Barnes I am sure that you checked everything out and, as usual, we are ready to go?" A not so reassuring "yes" was all that I could say.

We started engines about 06:30 hours and I gave each engine's instruments a special going over — Mag: OK; Oil temp: OK; RPMS: where they were supposed to be at about 1/8 throttle; Hydraulic pressure: OK. Ready to taxi when we get the light.

I always sat just behind the pilot with a hand ready to provide whatever the pilot might have need of. Often, on a foggy takeoff I managed the throttles and fuel mixture controls.

We began our taxi, falling in line with some 22 other B-17s that were making their way to the takeoff point on the runway. This time, it was our turn to be flight leader so we were the first in line. Looking down into the fog, my skin began to crawl worse than it already was.

We could only see some 200 yards down the runway. It looked like the inside of a marshmallow as we began our roll. Even in the cold early morning, sweat was rolling down the inside of my flight suit. This would cause a serious problem when we reached 15,000 feet or more. The sweat would freeze and I would be in deep trouble.

At 120 mph ground speed, Mac began a careful, slow pull on the controls, begging the plane to show that it wanted to fly. At 127 mph, the rumble of the landing gear dampened and the flow of air across the surfaces took hold. We were airborne.

Each plane began its roll 30 seconds apart and as soon as it was airborne, climbed out in a planned pattern, hoping the fog would not be too heavy and that we would break out of it between 3,000 feet and not more than 5,000 feet.

This morning the fog god was not very friendly. It was just over 9,000 feet before we saw the beginnings of the first light of day. I told myself, "This is not going to be a good day." No day was a good day to be flying into the enemy's fortress where one could easily get killed.

The tail gunner, Danielson, turned on the form-up light for the rest of the planes in our flight. Each squadron had a specific colored light for that group. All of the following planes were supposed to take their assigned place in the formation as soon as they could and begin the course to the target following the lead plane.

It was a long, trying climb to the flight altitude of 32,000 feet and some 50/60 degrees of frozen sky. Our course took us over the Netherlands, then we entered German's air space and went on to Berlin. Each gun position was ordered to test-fire their 50-caliber machine guns to make sure they would work at the extreme altitude and none of the crew had to be reminded to wear flak jackets.

About 20 minutes into German territory, the first of the German fighters began to attack the trailing group. Danielson began to call out one, then two B-17s falling out of formation. Then, in a very prayerful tone, he reported that one just exploded and he saw no chutes. He continued to keep the crew informed on the different Messerschmitt 109s' approaches to the bombers.

All too soon, our plane was the center of their attention and the tail gunner let loose with his two 50s. Then, the two waist gunners joined in to defend the plane. I was able to take on two Messerschmitt 109s diving from above and behind our plane. One broke into a smoke cloud but I didn't see it go down. I was to busy firing at several others that were beginning their attack. My smoker would be credited as a probable.

The fighters attacked in many different ways. This morning they came at us from high astern and dove through the squadron firing as they passed. Each 109 had a 20mm cannon in the nose and four 30mm machine guns in the wings. The cannons were fired just out of the range of our 50-caliber guns so we just had to sit and take it for a few frightening seconds until the range closed.

Their 20mm shells did not have exploding fuses but when they hit, the damage was extensive. As the fighters passed each gun position, waist, ball and turret guns would fire as long as the fighter was in range. We scored a number of hits. Only one of the fighters caught fire and the brown chute of the pilot could be seen. I guess he made it out and most likely we would see him another day.

After the first real attack on our plane, I took a quick look down the aft waist gun positions and the gunners were ankle deep in expended shells. I began to think we would not have enough ammo for the return attacks as we made our way home.

As our squadron's assigned target came into view, the bombardier called out, "Coming up on the IP! Beginning the bomb run." With the autopilot engaged, the bombardier took over the flight from his bombsight. The bomb bay doors were opened and our most vulnerable moment began.

At that moment, strangest thing then happened. Some of the most beautiful music I have ever heard came over our earphones. We asked the radioman if he was fooling with the radio and he said that he had not touched any of the dials. Just then, Danielson, our tail gunner, yelled, "I've been hit!"

We were in the critical moment of releasing our bombs, so the pilot asked him if he could hold on until we completed the run. Danielson said he would try. After our bombs had been released, we called back to Danielson and did not receive an answer.

The bombardier was assigned as our doctor. He found a large piece of flak had torn thru the bottom of Danielson's turret and cut a big gash out of his thigh. We carefully pulled him out of his tight gun position and Miskin (the bombardier) applied a tourniquet and compression bandage on the gaping wound to try and stop the bleeding. With Danielson's flight suit on (it was 50 degrees below zero) it was of little use.

Mishkin did all that he could do under the most difficult of circumstances. I could not but help think that the beautiful music was the angels calling Danielson home. R. B. Danielson, tail gunner from Nebraska, was dead. He died before we reached our home base.

There is no way to express the pain and hurt you feel when you lose a friend, especially one that

you trained with from the very beginning. There is never a replacement in our hearts and minds when a crewmember is lost.

As we approached Polebrook, I fired the red flare to let the base know that we had wounded on board. An ambulance met our plane as we came to a stop at the end of the runway and the base medics gently placed Danielson on a stretcher and put him in the ambulance. He would be sorely missed.

We had been at the right hand of death from the beginning of our first mission, but to see one of our crew get it really brought home just how close to death we all were.

IN MEMORY AND HONOR OF:

AIRMAN R. B. DANIELSON, TAIL GUNNER
Killed in action on November 16, 1944.

It would be impossible to name any airman or crew to respectfully honor and make a meaningful dedication of all that I have written. Therefore, it is my wish that my service in the 351st Bomb Group be dedicated to the 52,000 fellow airmen who did not return and lie in many far-flung graves.

There is never anything that any of us could ever say about our crewmates with whom we had lived with for months, trained for many long hours, sat and shared chow, told of home and family, girl friends and even had a few together. Now that they have lost their lives in the struggle to free most of the world, all we can do is remember and be grateful that we shared some of the most frightening times our youth.

MISSION #23
Misburg, Germany
November 29, 1944

Misburg is a suburb of Hanover and our target for this mission. We were becoming used to the northern route, the Zuider Zee and the turn into the target.

Flak was unusually intense and accurate. There were no clouds but it was very hazy.

We seemed to be losing more and more planes with each new mission.

MISSION #24
Lutzenkendorf, Germany
November 30, 1944

The target at Lutzekendorf was another synthetic oil plant. Our bombing accuracy was good

The two waist gunners, respectively, right gunner, A. F. Jones, was from the center of our country, North Platte, Nebraska; next on the left of the photo is our left gunner, E. J. Zourski of Massachusetts. The crewmember in the tail gun position is the replacement for R. B. Danielson, who was killed in action.

and there would be no oil products from that plant for some time, if ever.

As usual, the flak was murder at the target site.

MISSION #25
Leipzig, Germany
December 5, 1944

The wake up call was unusually early for this day's mission. Seldom were we awakened at 01:00 and it deepened our concerns about our chance of survival. As I staggered out to the breakfast of French toast and coffee, I was having a difficult time rationalizing my personal outcome for the remaining ten missions.

It was a matter of physical, mental and emotional stress that had really gotten to me. No human mind or body was supposed to go through such hell. We had been flying into Germany, dodging flak and fighting off the dammed German fighters for 25 missions and not been touched.

As the war dragged on, the German fighters had become more determined to destroy our bomber efforts, regardless of the target. At the morning briefing, the base commander gave us the word, "Target for today is Leipzig. (Our hearts dropped.) There are several important oil refineries on the outskirts of the city and we are going to blast them off the face of the German map!"

The colonel could get pretty carried away when he was not going on a mission. He put everything into the day's briefing, telling us how important it was that we do a good job.

Leipzig was deep into the heart of Germany and south of Berlin. The refineries were one of the most protected targets we'd had to face. The Germans let us know that we would be paying one hell of a price for trying to bomb the area. There would be a lot of extra flak and every German fighter plane that was still serviceable would be in the air to meet us as we started our bomb run.

Long before we were close to Berlin, the hard fight began. Messerschmitt 109s by the hundreds, Fockewulfs fighters by the dozen and a variety of twin-engine planes came at us from every direction. We would have to fight our way into the target area and then fight our way back out again. We'd have to keep fighting until we crossed into the English Channel. This would not be a good day.

We began our bomb run right on course and schedule. Just at the bomb release, we caught several damaging bursts of heavy flak that knocked out two engines and set them on fire. We had been bombing from 26,000 feet when we were hit. It was a long way home.

The pilot put the plane into a steep dive in order to attempt to put the fire out. There is nothing that scares the devil out of you more than being in a plane that dives from that altitude while its number-four engine is on fire and the plane still has lots of 100-octane fuel on board. We were diving almost straight down with the onrushing ground staring each of us in the face.

We were sure that we had bought the farm and it wasn't even our farm. At 5,000 feet, the dive had blown the fire out and we leveled off at treetop level to, hopefully, avoid any remaining German fighters as we hobbled our way across Germany, Belgium, Holland and the Channel. The Germans must have thought we crashed, because none attacked us on the return journey.

The Channel allowed us to take our first deep breath, and gave us some measure of hope that we would soon be safely back at our base. We were still about 500 feet over the Channel waters and the White Cliffs of Dover were staring us in the face. Slowly we began to climb in

order to have enough altitude to clear the cliffs at about 3,000 feet.

About ten miles from England, and still over the cold water of the Channel, two of the remaining engines began to miss and cut out. In a second, I called for emergency procedures to begin and for emergency landing instructions. I set the remaining engine at full throttle to the firewall.

We knew with full throttle on the one engine our time in the air was limited. We had just one choice … to glide to the base and pray loud and a heck of a lot so everyone and anyone could hear.

The runway at the base was almost straight in on the flight path we were on, so we headed straight into it. Just as we were about to cross the approach end of the runway, the one remaining engine stopped dead. We were at stall speed before the engine stopped. Now, with all engines out we would drop like a heavy rock.

I had already put the landing gear down. As we smashed into the runway, the gear folded up into the wing and we slid across the runway, breaking into a ball of fire.

I knew that all the numbers I had counted on were about to end in one big bang. As the plane slowed down enough for us to gather our survival thoughts, the first one to start getting out was the bombardier. His home on the plane was in the nose and he had to come by me in order to escape to the outside.

As he crashed into me, he banged against my leg and woke me from the stupor I was in and I came out of the haze. The bombardier was short and a little chubby and I was afraid he would get stuck in the bomb bay, so I jumped in front of him and kicked the aft side door open, hitting the ground at one heck of a run, going out across the field and as far away from the burning plane as I could get.

Somewhere, out in the middle of the field, an ambulance raced alongside me. A medic shouted, "Get in!"

Several of us who were running together shouted, "We need to get farther away from the plane before it blows up!" We had seen, and been part of many other such emergency crashes and watched helplessly as the plane exploded into hundreds of pieces. We wanted no part of those statistics!

MISSION #26
Aschaffenburg, Germany

Aschaffenburg was another long mission, some 8 hours. It was the main tank depot and supremely important to the German army. The

Seldom did any crewmembers survive such a crash. (I was lucky; I survived my one experience.) Below is a photo of the remains of a B-17 that crashed and burned. (We were so lucky!)

city was 20 miles southeast of Frankfort on the Main River.

MISSION #27
Frankfurt, Germany
December 9, 1944

Each mission to Frankfort was one of the most costly in lost planes. There were more than 400 batteries of flak in the main target area and they cost us dearly.

MISSION #28
Merseberg, Germany
December 11, 1944

Merseberg is another long flight and another major oil refinery. The German fighters had become fierce in their attacks and the flak batteries dealt a killing blow to our formations.

Flight time was 8 hours and 30 minutes.

MISSION #29
Bielefield, Germany
December 12, 1944

Bielefied was one of the key ordinance depots and as such, a key objective. When our bomb run was complete, no depot remained.

The flak was about the same as when bombing most important targets, but we did a good job destroying it.

Flight time was 5 hours and 30 minutes.

MISSION #30
HARBURG, GERMANY
December 15, 1944

Oil refineries were at the top of our target list and there was a big refinery at Harburg. It is a southern suburb of Hanburg. Just as at Hanburg, the flak was intense and extremely accurate. We are getting more tense and nervous because we are near to completing our 35 missions.

Flight time 7 hours.

MISSION #31
Kassel, Germany
December 22, 1944

More marshaling yards, but this time we caught many trains in the yard. When we departed the area, there were almost none. We also knew that the yard would be repaired in just a few days with more trains running again.

Flying time 7 hours and 45 minutes.

MISSION #32
Koblenz, Belgium
December 24, 1944

The briefing officer slowly lifted the cover that hid the day's planned mission. It was to Koblenz and at only 16,000 feet instead of 30,000 feet. This was our 32nd mission and it was one of those days when even a German duck should not be flying.

The long line of B-17s was like ghosts in the early morning fog. The planes seemed to disappear as they began their roll down the blacktop of the runway. Our plane was in line waiting its turn to roll.

Two of the earlier B-17s, about the 5th or 6th, left the runway. As they swung around so that they could find their place and form up, they collided with a roar at about 300 feet. They must have overflown each other. There was one heck of a blast as the fuel, bombs and crew disintegrated just beyond the end of the field. We could do nothing but continue our part of the mission. The tension is at its worst due to the two-plane explosion that happened right in front of us.

Our four Wright cyclone 1820 engines were at top performance, yet as I began the advance of the throttles, they complained at being forced to the maximum. We began our roll and soon became airborne. It seemed like it took forever before we broke out of the fog somewhere about 3,000 feet. The crew welcomed the bright sunlight. The plane seemed to gain a few extra feet of altitude as the crew breathed a great sigh of relief.

Dropping the right wing just a fraction, we turned to find our assigned position in the squadron and the wing. There were some 1,000 planes in the air at once, all headed for some part of Germany. Each group had a target and as the flight crossed into the target area, formations would break off and head for their respective assignments.

Sometimes, there would be four different targets for the entire flight. This was done with the hope of confusing the German fighters. It would also scatter the fighters in several different directions so that no one group would have the entire brunt of a fighter attack.

On to Koblenz

December is the serious beginning of winter in all parts of Europe. As usual, clouds formed all around the planned route command had given us. At 12,000 feet, the crew went on oxygen. At 15,000 feet the bright contrails began to tell everyone we were headed into harm's way. The Germans were making every possible attempt to blast the B-17s from the sky as they made their last ditch push and defense.

Koblenz is in Belgium and the push was what became known as the Battle of the Bulge. Our target was to bomb the concentrations of big guns, trucks and all supply convoys in the area. Our bomb load was "anti-personnel bombs." When they hit and exploded, they cut everything within range of the blast. Trees were shredded; vehicles, light tanks and men became just pieces.

Our orders were to bomb from 16,000 feet to make sure that our bombs landed directly on target so they would do the most damage. Our approach to the target brought an unbelievable amount of heavy black deadly flak into our path.

It was so heavy that it seemed one could walk through it.

As we made our way to the IP, there was one heck of a blast. We had been hit in our left outboard engine and it was on fire. Then the left inboard engine burst into flame, too. Fuel was flowing out of the fuel cells and it would be only seconds before it reached the red-hot supercharger. It was time to bail out, and fast!

If you have never bailed out before, it's no real thrill, especially when it's over enemy territory. The crew was going out from every possible exit. There was a hatch beside my station. When the exit ring was pulled, the hatch would fly out and away from the plane.

I pulled the ring. There were no seconds to ponder if this was the right thing to do. I instantly tumbled out of the hatch. One might think about life at a time like this, but there were only two choices: either stay in the plane and be blown to pieces or take the chance of capture by the Germans. *The Germans can only shoot me,* I thought.

I had not fallen free of the plane by more than 5 seconds when it disappeared in a ball of fire and completely disintegrated. I guess that I had fallen about 3,000 feet when I pulled the D-ring of my chute. The big white blossom of the canopy looked great above my head.

Jones, our waist gunner, had gone out of his gun port and we floated down to ground together. There was some comfort knowing that I would have a crewmate to share whatever awaited us. We landed in a soft, rain soaked field with shocks of grain scattered about.

There was a barn some 100 yards from our landing. We hid the chutes in a hedgerow, out of sight, and made for the barn in one heck of a hurry. We new the Germans were not too far behind. (We had landed some 20 miles inside the German line.)

Bending as low as we could, Jones and I headed for the barn and climbed up into the loft. As I looked about, our muddy footprints were like a map to the place we were hiding. We looked at the prints and realized the barn would be the first place the Germans would look for us and we had left them footprints to follow.

Hurrying back down the ladder, we looked out across the field. There were dozens of hay shocks standing there and we picked one next to the stone barn's wall as our hiding place.

The farmers shock their grain by tying it in bundles and stacking it with the grain heads up. They form a circle about 10 feet in diameter with the center somewhat open. As the shock reaches three or four layers, the top is folded in to make a kind of peak with the grain head sticking up. It seemed to dry out better this way.

Regardless of the farmer's method of harvesting, we gently pushed our way inside the center of a stack, pulling shut the small entry hole once we were inside. Both Jones and I felt exposed to the German soldiers that were bound to come looking. Since the earth was soft under the shocks, we scooped out as much of it as we could so as to lower our bodies as far down as possible.

All too soon, we heard a Jeep drive up. The soldiers followed the footprints up into the hayloft. We could hear them jabbing the hay with the forks. They went up into the barn saying, "Kum out! Kum out!" No one came out, so they went down to the farmhouse.

We could hear them hollering and screaming down there. I didn't know what they were saying but knew it wasn't good. Then they came back and went up into the hayloft and machine-gunned everything.

Next, they walked around the barn and machine-gunned everything. When they came to the grain stacks, they shot into our hiding place. All we could do was shut our eyes and wait for the bullets to hit our bodies.

The rounds tore through the stack just fractions of inches above our uniforms. When you are young and scared you get low in that haystack! I was worried the bullets might set the hay on fire. How we were not hit is beyond my understanding. Again, God must have been protecting us.

As a last resort, the Germans jabbed their bayonets as far into the hay as they could and then went back to the barn to ask the farmer if he had seen two parachutists. After a couple of hours, the soldiers left.

After they left, the French people came out. They were trying to get us to come out, but we were afraid if we did they would just turn us over to the Germans. We did not dare move and stayed frozen both in fear and cold. The hay gave us some protection from the bitter cold weather but not much.

There was no conversation between Jones and me; there was no need. We stayed hidden for three days. With hunger and the increased cold making us just about as miserable as we could ever get, some measure of sleep was had, but only because we were so exhausted.

On about the third day, we heard strong voices coming our way and didn't know if they were German or not. We could make out the sound of tanks and decided we'd better surrender or we were going to die from the elements.

With our hands held high above our heads, we began to walk towards the tank sounds in our muddy clothing, keeping the house and the barn between us. When we finally sighted the tanks, they were going east and had big white stars painted on their sides.

The tanks were part of General Patton's 3rd Army advance scouts! The General was driving the Germans back into Germany. We began to wave as widely as we could, keeping our hands held high over our heads.

I waved to the lead tank and he stopped, looked down at us, and seemed bewildered by our muddy appearance. We told the tanker about our sad experience and identified ourselves. The tank commander told us to keep walking on the road back the way they had come and we would find the rest of the U. S. Army.

He radioed back to let someone know that two cruddy flyers were walking their way and asked them to give us a hand. It wasn't long before a jeep came roaring up to ask if we were lost. *(There is always a smart ass everywhere you go!)*

The driver was a young looking lieutenant. He asked us to get in, saying he would take us back to the rear of the war. We were driven to a small air base and flown back to England in a C-47 to finish our part of the war.

That was one Christmas that I will *never* forget.

MISSION #34
Koblenz. Belgium
December 30, 1944.

Back to the marshaling yards. It was extremely important to keep all supplies coming from Germany from reaching the German troops that were attacking the Belgium Bulge area. We really did a number on the yard also.

Flying time 7.00 hours.

MISSION #35
Meyen, Germany
January 2, 1945

This was the one we had been working for … our last mission! The target at Meyen is a small town, 15 miles west of Koblenz and on the main supply route to the Bulge. We had a new first pilot due to our pilot having finished his 35th mission on our last flight.

The ME-262 jets attacked us again and it was all we could do to keep our cool. One of the waist gunners said, "If they shoot us down today, I am really going to be mad." What he had done was take all the extra flak jackets and made himself a bed out of the jackets to keep the flak from getting to him.

When the bombardier announced, "Bombs away!" our hearts began to beat at their normal rhythm. All we had to do was get back to our base and kiss the ground for the last time.

When we finally landed, pulled up and parked, all of the crew jumped out, kissed mother earth and said, "I don't care if I ever get into another airplane again!" And that is the way it ended.

Flying time was 7.00 hours.

35 MISSIONS AT A GLANCE

08/27/44	BERLIN	10/05/44	PLAUEN	12/05/44	LEIPSIG
08/30/44	PEENEMUNDE	10/07/44	STETTIN*	12/09/44	ASCHAFFENBURG
09/09/44	KEIL	10/14/44	COLOGNE	12/11/44	FRANKFORT
09/10/44	LUDWIGSHAVEN	10/15/44	RHULAND	12/12/44	BIEFEID
09/12/44	DULMAN*	10/17/44	HANNOVER*	12/15/44	HARBURG
09/17/44	MERSEBERG	10/22/44	COLOGNE	12/22/44	KASSEL
09/19/44	MUNSTER	10/25/44	HAMBERG	12/24/44	KOBLENZ*
09/25/44	FRANKFORT	10/26/44	GELSENNKIRCHEN	12/30/44	KAISERLAUTERN
09/26/44	ESCHWEILER	10/30/44	MUNSTER	01/01/45	KOBLENZ
09/27/44	COLOGNE	11/16/44	BERLIN**	01/02/45	MEYEN
10/02/44	KASSEL	11/29/44	MISBURG		
10/03/44	STERKRADE	11/30/44	LUTZKENDORF		

*Worst missions
**Tail Gunner R.B. Danielson killed in action.

DEALING WITH LOSSES AND STRESS

One time the weather was horrible. We were lucky to come in. We were over the airfield but we couldn't see it. We couldn't see the runway!

Finally the bombardier spotted it. He cried, "There it is! There it is!" Man we just dove onto it. It was the wrong end, but we got down.

We took the plane over to its place and parked it. We did all the maintenance reports that had to be done and went on to interrogation. After that, we went over to the mess hall.

The mess hall had pork chops that night. After a ten-hour flight, you are hungry. They only gave me one when I went through the line. I said, "Man, give me a couple of them things. They're not very big."

The cook said, "There aren't very many and we've got to have enough for everybody."

I said, "There are only three aircraft that made it back. There will be lots of them leftover."

The cook relented and said, "Help yourself."

I ate four of them little fellers.

When you came back after a mission and several airplanes had been lost, the barracks would be partly empty. The next day, though, here would come the new crews.

After this mission, four different new crews came into the barracks. They looked and saw all the empty bunks around and said, "These guys go home?"

I said, "Yes, they went home. This one, he went down on his 5th mission. This crew went down on their 3rd and this crew over here went down on their first."

One of the new guys asked me, "How many missions have you got?"

I said, "Well, we're still here, so we haven't finished." I didn't tell him how many we had and they didn't know what to think. I said, "You don't

> *"The hardest part after flying a mission was coming back and seeing all the empty bunks back in the barracks."*
> — Carl Barnes

go home from here very often. Their home is up with St. Peter. That's how we got those empty bunks."

Lot of guys would come in hollering "Fresh blood!" That wasn't the best way to start. It gave you a bad feeling. But, we survived. The doctor would give us a drink after each flight so we wouldn't end up a Section 8. That is what would bring you down — seeing all the empty bunks. It don't take too long looking at the empty bunks to give you a Section 8.

I think I would have had one, if the doctor hadn't caught me and made sure I took my medicine. I was right on the verge. I didn't drink; there were enough drunkards in my family. I thought I wasn't supposed to drink. When you came back from a flight they would give you a double shot of whiskey.

Well, one day I came back and it had been a rough mission. As you headed into interrogation, the doctor would look you over and he could tell, I guess. He came over to me and said, "What's the matter son? You don't look too sharp."

I said, "Man, they're getting rougher. They are going to get us."

He asked, "Well, have you been taking your whiskey?"

I said, "No, I don't drink."

He said, "Don't think of it as drinking. Think of it as medicine. And if you don't take it, you won't make it. You'll have a nervous breakdown and get the whole crew shot down."

He took me over to the counter and ordered two double shots. I thought I was going to drink one and he would drink the other. But after I drank one he handed me the other one and said, "Drink this one, too."

The bombardier was the same way. He didn't drink. He would drink the double shots and then get over to interrogation and the interrogation officer would ask "Did you see anything new today?"

He would be drunk already and say, "Those SOBs are trying to kill us. They were shooting right at us."

That night, I went over to the mess hall and ate and then went to bed. I guess I passed out, because about 9 or 10 p.m. the Germans came over to visit us. They bombed the hanger and shot up five airplanes — caught them on fire and burned them up. I slept right through it.

I woke up late the next morning and when I got up, the barracks was empty. I was too late to go to the mess hall, so I went to the canteen to get something to eat. The British ran it ... so they had tea and crumpets and that sort of thing.

As I ate breakfast, I heard everyone talking about the bombing. I was all ears and asked, "What bombing?"

The canteen guy said, "Where were you guys last night? Didn't you see the Germans come over? They were bombing us and shooting up everything. They burned up five airplanes!"

As I ate my breakfast and drank my tea, I hopped on my bicycle and headed down to the flight line to see what really happened. Sure enough, wing tips and tails were all that was left of the five planes that were hit. Next, I went over

the hanger. It had caught fire and the planes and one end of the hanger had burned.

After seeing all that, I went back to the barracks. By that time some people had come back in. "Why didn't you wake me up so I could get in the bomb shelter?" I asked them. "What if they'd hit our barracks?"

They said, "We tried to wake you up, but you were dead. They couldn't have killed you any deader."

So this was the only we'd been bombed while I was stationed there, and I missed it.

After that, I'd take my double shots and you can't believe how it would calm me down. I was tight with stress. I'd been on oxygen all day, under stress of flak and fighters and then to come back and fight the weather to get in. I was exhausted. I'd take those shots and just relax, eat and go to bed and then just drop off to sleep. The next morning I'd be able to take off again. So, I completed my 35 missions that way.

PROCESSED OUT AND HEADED HOME

They processed us out real quick so they could have room for the new crews that were coming in. We went through our base and checked out, then on to Stone, England, where we had come when we first arrived.

We were there for several days waiting for a ship that would take us back to the states. We went to Liverpool and they put us on the *Queen Mary* that had been converted to a troop ship. It had a lot of wounded hospital patients on board. The guys that could get around were assigned to one of the wounded men who could not get around. They were to take care of them and get them into a lifeboat if a German submarine should hit the ship with a torpedo.

At long last, we left Liverpool and headed north between the Atlantic and the Irish Sea, out of

Belfast then out into the open sea. The open sea was really rough. I was on the promenade deck in the bar area where they had bunks bolted to the deck. I had my legs wrapped around my bunk, with my hands locked under them in order to stay in my bunk.

It did not take long before I was seasick and had to get out on deck. I ran for the railing and worked my way aft to the stern of the ship where I stayed for two days.

We had two destroyer escorts and we could see them pop up every now and then. Finally the captain of our ship said the destroyers were going back because they could not take the bad weather. He said that we didn't have to worry because the German subs could not surface in the storm.

Carl on leave with his grandfather, Luther Steven Barnes.

After we got far enough from land, we went south. The ship was always zigzagging to evade subs. They picked up sounds of submarines twice. We had to sleep in full dress with life jackets close by because of this.

It was a fast ship so the crossing was quick. Two days before we arrived in New York, a PBY was above us to protect us from any further threats from subs. Finally, the ship came into the port of New York and the Statue of Liberty stood there to greet us. It was a beautiful sight for us to come home to.

As we departed the ship, the Red Cross met us with donuts, coffee and other food. We were then put on buses that took us to the New Jersey side. There we were processed out for transportation to our home area.

They had a huge steak dinner with all the trimmings for us in New Jersey. We were mad at the Red Cross for feeding us all those donuts and spoiling our appetites.

After some three days, we were put on a troop train and headed west. We went from New Jersey to Chicago. Every so often, they would let some of the troops off.

Finally, we arrived at Camp Beale in Northern California. I went home for a short visit, and then my next stop was a convalescent hospital.

FINISHING UP

I was at the hospital for a month, and then I was reassigned to a B-29 school at Chanute Field in Illinois. Regulations set in! First I was assigned to a B-29 class, then we had to march to and from each place we went: chow, classrooms, etc.

The second morning it was really cold. My feet had been frozen on our 16th mission in England so they would not take much cold. On the second day, marching to class, I just collapsed. They called an ambulance and hauled me to the base hospital to see what was wrong. The hospital had my records and it showed my feet had been frozen. So, they put my feet in a hot water bath. I had to do this every morning, so that ended my B-29 class.

I was then sent to Scott Field in southern Illinois, right across from the river in St. Louis, Missouri. I spent the rest of my Army Air Force career at Scott Field flying co-pilot on C-47s and training radio operators.

We would fly two flights a day, one in the morning and the other in the afternoon. We would go up and the radio operators would practice radio contacts with different points and try to navigate by radio. It was a pretty good duty and I enjoyed it.

After the Japanese surrendered and the war was over, the Air Force began to let us out. I had enough points to be discharged with the first batch because of the number of points I had accumulated by being overseas, in combat, and earning a lot of medals (5 points per medal). I got out and came home to California.

The 8th Army Air Force

GENERAL INFORMATION

- The total number of B-17s flown from England from 1942 through to the end of the war with Germany in April 1945 has not been released…but it was in the thousands.

- We do know the approximate number of airmen lost in all commands of the Army Air Force. It was a staggering 52,000. Each B-17 was manned by a crew of 10. Thus with a total of 52,000 casualties divided by a crew of 10 yields over 5,200 B-17s that were used in combat.

- The Eighth Air Force ended World War II with the highest casualty rates of any Allied force. In the process of conducting this bombing campaign, it played the major role in disrupting Germany's war economy and transportation system.

THE 351ST BOMB GROUP

- 8600 Missions
- 175 B-17s lost due to combat & related causes
- 1,750 crew members killed or missing in action
- Squadrons included the 508th, 509th, 510th and 511th all based at Polebrook.

"The price these men paid few care about at this late date in our country's history," Carl Barnes said in 1999. "They seem not to care the price that was paid for the liberty and freedoms that we enjoy today."

A Day with the 351st

by Preston Long

Breakfast at one, briefing at two
You're flying today; you'll hit the blue.
These few words that we hear so soon
Brings us from bed and we scramble for room,
As each single man goes a different way.
We are griping. They woke us early today.
Finally we are dressed and out for a snack.
Even this may sound too good to be true,
To some little guy who's never been up at two.
But to me it's a life that I lead each day.
We're winning this war, who cares which way.
Jolly Old England they call this place.
Let a G.I. name it, you'll make a face.
We trudge in the mud to the briefing room,
Still rubbing our eyes, they woke us too soon.
We have left our valuables; in good hands they stay,

For no one knows the dangers of today.
But still we know we're fighting a war
For a place we love that's not very far.
We learn our target, we clean our guns,
Who Knows? We might shoot some Huns.
Take off is scheduled at a time they set,
And out at the plane, the crew has met
For a final chat and a roll on the ground,
Then we take off, Germany bound.
We reach that altitude where the air is thin.
Oxygen mask on, the crew checks in.
Now it is day and the sun shines bright
Your mind wanders away to that furlough night.
Finally the target and the flak gets thick.
Hang on Pilot, steady on that stick
You hear "Bombs Away" and the ship gives a bound
You turn off the target, Homeward Bound.

You look down below and there's really a sight
And you know darn well "Jerry" won't sleep tonight.
As the home base is reached, you peel off and land.
They all came back; Thank God. Every man.
As this I done over and over each day
You see what you are fighting for ...
An endless peace and a Brighter Day.

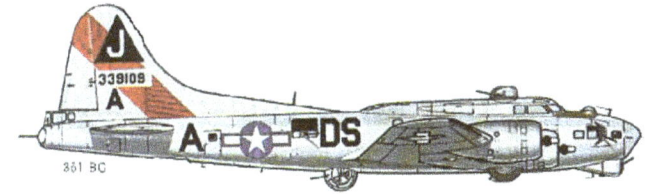

Carl C. Barnes Assigned Eighth AF: April 43

351 ST BOMBARDMENT GROUP (H)

WING & COMMAND ASSIGNMENTS

VIII BC, 1 BW, 101 PCBW: May 43.

VIII BC, 1 BD, 1 CBW: 13 Sep. 43.

VIII BC, 1 BD, 92 CBW: 1 Nov. 43.

VIII BC, 1 BD, 94 CBW: 15 Dec. 43.

1 BD, 94 CBW: B Jan. 44.

1 AD, 94 CWB: 1 Jan. 45.

COMPONENT SQUADRONS

50Bth, 509th, 51 0th and 511 th Bombardment Squadron (H).

COMBAT AIRCRAFT

B-17F (from blocks 75-BO, 25-DL and VE); B-17G.

STATION

POLEBROOK 15 April 43-23 Jun. 45
(Air echo from 15 April 43. Ground echo in c. 12 Mav 43).

THE MIGHTY EIGHTH

GROUP COS

Col William A. Hatcher Jr:

Col Eugene A. Romig:

Col Robert W. Burns:

Col Merlin I. Carter:

FIRST MISSION: 14 May 43. Last Missions: 311.

TOTAL CREDIT SORTIES: B,600.

TOTAL. BOMB TONNAGE: 20,357 (43 tons leaflets) .

A/E MIA: 124. E/A CLAIMS: 303-49-177.

MAJOR AWARDS: Two Distinguished Unit Citations: 9 Oct. 43: Anklam. 11 Jan. 44 (All 1 st BD groups).

CLAIMS TO FAME

• 509BS made 54 consecutive missions Jun. 43·Jan. 44 without loss.

• "Ball Boys" squadron (511 BS) was part of Group.

• Clark Gable flew missions w.th this group. .

EARLY HISTORY

Activated 1 Oct. 42 at Salt Lake City AB, Utah. Established at Geiger Fd, Wash. in Nov. 42 where Group was assembled for initial training. Second phase training at Biggs Fd, Tex. between Dec. 42 and Mar. 43. Pueblo AAB. Col. for preparation for overseas movement. Ground echelon left Pueblo for New York C. 12 Apr. 43. Air echelon began movement C. 1 Apr. 43.

SUBSEQUENT HISTORY

Redeployed USA May/Jun. 45. First alc left 21 May 45. Ground echelon sailed for US on 25 Jun. 45 aboard Queen Elizabeth. Docked 30 Jun. 43. Personnel 30 days R & R. Assembled Sioux Falls AAFd, SO. Jul. 45 but Group inactivated 28 Aug. 45. Activated as a Minuteman missile wing in 1963 and established at Whiteman AFB, Mo.

508TH

509TH

510TH

511TH

Military Awards Received by Carl C. Barnes

Air Medal — 7
European, African, Middle Eastern Campaign

Bronze Stars — 5
Presidential Unit Citation
European Victory Medal
Korean S.V. Medal
United Nations SV Medal
National Defense Medal
World War II Medal

Presidential Citation
351st List of information

T/sgt CARL C. BARNES   18156793   *   *   *

BATTLE HONORS- Citations of Units---Sec. XI
*   *   *   *   *

     XI. BATTLE HONORS.--1 As authorized by Executive Order No. 9396, (sec. I, WD. 1942), superseding Executive Order No. .9075 (Sec III, Bull. 11,WD, 1942), Citation of the following unit by the Commanding General, Eighth Air Force, in General Orders, No 355, 11 May 1944, under the provisions of section 1V, Circular No. 333, War Department, T43, in the name of the President of the United States as public evidence of deserved honor and distinction, is confirmed.
The citation reads as follows.follows:

The 1st Bombardment Division (H) is cited for extraodinary heroism, determination, and esprit de corps in action against the enemy on 11 January 1944, On this occasion the 1st Bombardment Division led the entire Eighth Air Force penetration into central Germany to attack vital aircraft factories. After assembly was accomplished and the formation was proceeding toward Germany, adverse weather conditions were encountered which prevented sffective fighter cover from reaching the 1st Bombardment Division. Taking full advantage of the relative vulnerability of the lead division, the enemy concentrated powerful forces against it. The scale of the enemy attack is graphically indicated by the fact that 400 encounters with enemy aircraft were recorded by units of the 1st Bombardment Division. The gunners met these continuous attacks with accurate fire and the division continued toward the targets as briefed where bombs were dropped with excellent results. On the return trip the enemy continued to concentrate his efforts on the 1st Bombardment Division. Figures of enemy aircraft claimed by our gunners indicate that the heroism of this division inflicted heavy looses on the enemy in the air as well as on the ground. Two hundred and ten enemy aircraft, the largest number ever claimed by any division of the Eighth Air Force for any one mission, were confirmed as destroyed, 43 probably destroyed and 84 damaged. The division lost 42 heavy bombers and many of those which returned were heavily damaged. Four hundred and thirty officers and enlisted men failed to return, 2 were killed, and 32 others wounded.
The extraordinary heroism and tenacious fighting spirit demonstrated by the 1st Bombardment Division in accomplishing its assigned task under exceptionally difficult conditions reflect highest credit on this organization, The Army Air Forces, and the armed forces of the United States.

*   *   *   *   *

       By order of the Secretary of War:

                                    G. C. MARSHALL
                                    Chief of staff

OFFICIAL
J.A. ULIO
Major General
   The Adjutant General
A TRUE EXTRACT COPY
/s/ Roberts P. Johnson, Jr.
/t/ ROBERTS P. JOHNSON JR.
    Lieut. Colonel, AGD.

In Loving Memory
of Those Who Did Not Return

No greater love hath man, than to
Lay down his life for another.
In Berlin, Polesti, and along the Rhine
There lie the heros who were left behind.
Only their bodies were left there to die,
As God gave their souls new wings to fly.
Oh yes, we'll remember and honor these braves
We'll look with sorrow at many graves,
While our hearts we know so well,
Their battle is over and so is their hell.
Brave young men, the lives that you gave,
Were a gift to us all who are here today.
It was the greatest gift you had to give,
So each of us here, right now, could live.
Brave young men, we honor your memories today
"Well done thou good and faithful servants."

We must never forget our friends and comrades who made the supreme sacrifice and especially those that were missing in action and interred on foreign soil. Some of us have had the privilege of visiting the American Cemetery in Cambridge, England and have paid our honor and respect to those that lie there. The "Wall of Missing" lists the names of the individuals killed in action; their bodies never recovered for burial. It is truly a sobering scene and as thoughts drift back to the days of combat, it is not hard to realize that, "There but for the grace of God, go I." It could've been me...

— Carl C. Barnes

(Right) This monument is located at the end of the main runway that was used by the 351st Bomb Group during WWII. The inscription reads: In memory of the 351st Bombardment Group (Heavy) Eighth United States Army Air Force. 311 group combat bombing missions were flown from this airfield over occupied Europe, 1943–1945. 175 B-17 Flying Fortresses and their crews were lost. 303 enemy aircraft were destroyed in aerial combat. (Left) National Museum of the United States Air Force, Wright-Patterson Air Force Base, Greene County, Ohio,

CHAPTER 5

A Short Civilian Reprieve

1945–1951

After I got out, my first priority was to find a job. I saw the Rocky Mountain Drilling Company's ad in the Bakersfield newspaper. They were looking for help. I gave them a call and after a very short interview I was hired. I worked there for five years.

One Sunday, my Aunt Ruby Songer came to me and told me that the church she attended had special prayer meetings for all the local servicemen and that she had put my name on the list for prayer during the time I was flying over Germany. She asked if I would go to her church so the people could see first hand just who they had spent time praying for.

I went with my two cousins, Charles and Esty Songer. My cousin Charles introduced me to one of the attendees named Martha Marple. Later, we went to dinner and I had many dates with her. On June 14, 1947, we were married.

DOMESTIC BLISS

The first thing we did was buy a house on my G.I. Bill. I had some of my mustering out pay left, which we used to make a down payment on a refrigerator, gas stove, small table and chairs, and, of course, a bedroom set. That was how we started our life together.

About 16 months later, a daughter, Janet, joined our family. We had her room all fixed up, and as I took stock of my new world, I felt like something that I had never dared to dreamed of was coming true. I never thought that I would return home from my missions over Germany let alone get married. Now I had a wife and baby daughter. I continued my service in the Air Force with the reserves.

DUTY AND COUNTRY COME CALLING AGAIN

When Janet was about two years old, I received a letter from Uncle Sam. He was in

Troop ship on the way to Korea.

trouble again in a place called Korea. The letters from our Uncle said, "Report." I packed up a limited amount of personal items and was sent to McClellan Air Force Base near Sacramento, California.

We rented out our house in Bakersfield so Martha and Janet could move to Sacramento. We found a little, but nice apartment there.

I was flying out of Sacramento to many places all over the United States, hauling all kinds of freight. The freight was off-loaded at Travis AFB in Fairfield, California, and then loaded onto C-124s for shipment to the Tachacawa AFB in Japan.

I thought the duty was a good one. I enjoyed flying all over the United States, and seeing many parts of the country that I had only read about.

Then one day, returning from a flight, I had orders to go to Korea to do the same thing I was doing in California. I was to deliver items from Tachacawa into Korea and the South Pacific. So Mart moved back to Bakersfield and into our little house and I left out of San Francisco on a troop ship, the *USNS General John Pope*.

We were 11 days on the high seas. After the first couple of days, I became grew bored. I went to the galley and asked if they could use some help. The chief of the galley looked at my rank and said, "No, you got too high a rank."

I went back to our quarters and asked a corporal if he would trade me work jackets. I then went back to the galley and asked again. The chief asked, "Did you really want to work?"

I replied, "Yes. I'm really bored and needed something to pass the time."

I was assigned to the bakery shop and for the rest of the trip I baked bread and many other items. I also ate much better. When we docked in Yokohama, I got my jacket back from the corporal. He thanked me and said that he hadn't had any work details during the entire trip.

FLYING CARGO

From Yokohama we traveled by train to the southern most Japanese island of Kyushu and the city of Fukuoka. The base I was assigned to was an old Japanese air base renamed Brady Field. I was to fly C-46 cargo planes from Japan to Korea to deliver much needed war supplies. Our quarters were tents with wood floors and walls about four feet up the sides. Real cozy.

This turned out to be the same kind of duty I had before. The only difference was this time I was delivering war goods from Tachacawa to Korea and the general South Pacific area. We would fly in food, ammunition and other much-needed supplies and then fly out the servicemen who had been wounded or killed. There were times when we had to drop supplies to the ground troops as they moved up the peninsula. The Army finally moved to an old Japanese WWII base called K-2.

It wasn't too bad in Japan and Korea. Flying cargo did not place us in real combat, but many times we were in the shooting area. When we first got involved, the Chinese had pushed the UN troops down to the Seoul area. The Chinese and North Koreans had almost half of the Korean peninsula.

My crew's job was to support our ground troops by flying into airfields like K-2. The Chinese were on one end of the field and the UN troops were on the other. We had to fly down a canyon and land at K-2 which was an old Japanese airfield left over from WWII. As soon as we touched down, we had to reverse our props, stop real quick, and swing around to park behind a mound of dirt. The supplies were unloaded and as we were ready to leave, the UN field operations ran up a red flag.

Our Army was holed up in foxholes and as the red flag was raised, they would turn all their machine guns loose on the Chinese to keep their heads down so we could fly out of the field. We had to take off directly over the Chinese and swing back through the canyon as fast as we could in order to keep from being shot at. We could look down onto the Chinese positions and see them firing their rifles up at us as we passed over their heads.

Several times we decided to get even with them and took some hand grenades with us. When we were over them, we would pull the pins and toss the grenades out of the airplane window. It made us feel like we were doing a little fighting back. I don't know if we even hit anything or hurt anyone.

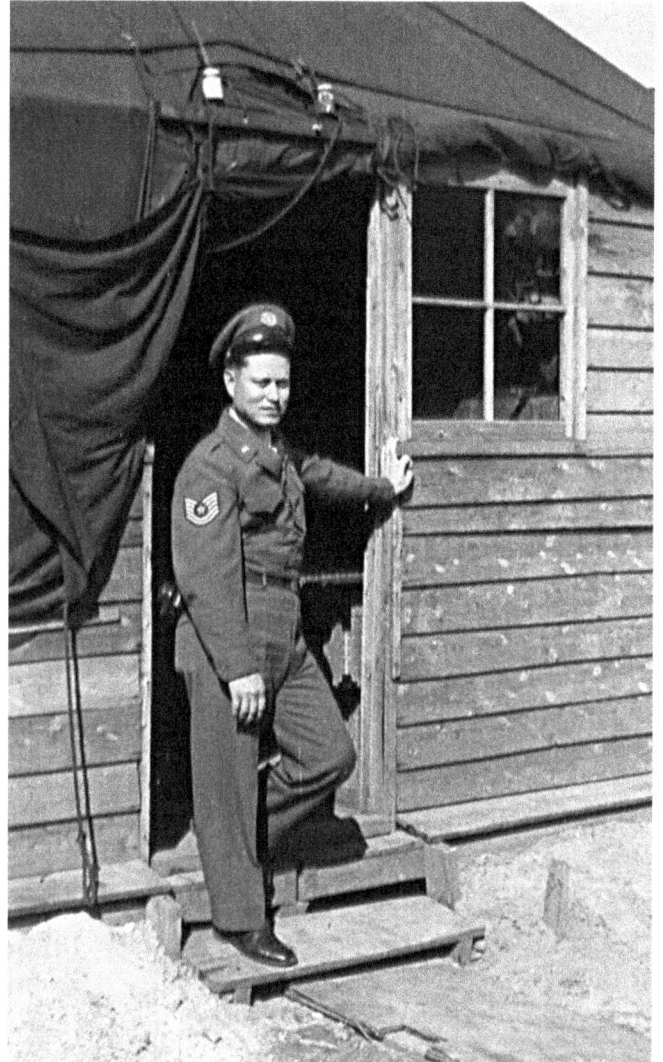

One time they got lucky and a shot hit the oil cooler in one of the engines. We were losing oil real bad. We had to go into Pusan on the southern tip of the Korean peninsula and radio Japan to send a new oil cooler on the next flight. We stayed in Pusan overnight. We got a new oil cooler the next day, changed it and flew back to Japan.

Our base was on a finger of land with water on both sides. When landing, we would come in over Fukuoka across the bay and land. Just out of Fukuoka was an F-80 fighter base. The F-80 base had radar. When the weather was bad, they would let us down in 1,000-foot intervals. We had to work our way down until we got down

under the storm and then we would fly across the bay to our base.

One time I had only one engine, so they let us down fast. As we headed across the bay, we were lined up on the taxiway instead of the runway. We had to make a go-around on one engine. I didn't know if the old C-46 would make it, but it did. We changed the engine and a couple days later we flew to Korea.

NOT COMBAT, BUT STILL DANGEROUS

It was raining and socked in. This was after the Air Force had taken over the based and they installed GCA (ground controlled approach). Coming in on one engine (we had lost the one engine that we had overpowered when landing in Japan), we flew down a canyon. It was cold but we were really sweating. We couldn't see anything; we just listened to the GCA.

Finally, GCA said, "You are 12 feet above the runway." We could see it by then. We landed, pulled of the runway, cleared and parked, then radioed Japan for another engine. We had to stay at that base for about a week. We took off the bad engine and replaced it with the new engine and then checked it out.

In the meantime, while taking the old engine off, a flight of Chinese planes came down the canyon shooting up the place. The Chinese planes came strafing, and I thought they were shooting right at us. They shot the barrels of fuel and caught them on fire. I saw the planes coming in and I dropped down off the engine stand and right into a foot of very cold water behind the C-46 wheel. After it was over, I looked around and decided that if they had hit the main wheel, it would have exploded and killed me … rather than any of the Chinese strafing machine gun bullets.

It was really cold in Korea during the winter. We had cots to sleep on but we had to put newspapers down under our sleeping bags to keep the cold from coming up through the cot. With the engine finally on and checked out, we flew back to Japan. On another flight, we had a new co-pilot. On our way back to Japan, we stopped in Pusan. It was on the southern tip of Korea. You flew across the harbor, then down a canyon and the runway was right along the side of a river. We would fly in, load up, do whatever we had to do, and then take off in the opposite direction out across and up the riverbank and across the harbor.

STORIES FROM FUKUOKA

Generally we flew together, calling out flaps … you go up 20 degrees, etc. … and as the air speed increases you take the flaps and come up another 10 degrees until they are all the way up. This guy, the new copilot, had called for flaps.

He just reached over and hit the flap switch and the flaps came all the way up. Down we went, sailing across the harbor.

We were so low that we were below some of the ships' masts in the harbor. I thought we were going right into the ocean. Finally, we attained enough air speed that we just barely made it across the harbor. We had 40 passengers in the back. They didn't know what was going on but we did up in the cockpit and we sure didn't want to fly with that guy again.

We lost several C-46s, usually at night ... they flew into a mountain near the bases.

We also got caught at our own base when a typhoon came roaring through. We lived in a tent city. The tents were boarded up 4 feet then the tent covered the frame. When the typhoon came through, it blew everything away. We had to evacuate everyone and the planes to the Philippines. We took four planes and returned with new tents to rebuild our tent city.

Fukuoka was a big city. We could still see a lot of destruction in the harbor leftover from the war. There were a lot of Japanese ships that had been bombed and sunk. Part of the ships would stick out of the water and some were burnt. Some of the Japanese cargo ships had been re-floated and were being rebuilt. We would watch the shipyard workers rebuilding them and it was kinda interesting.

When not on duty we would go out into the country and watch the farmers plowing their fields with

Landing at Okinawa.

water buffaloes. "Honey" buckets filled with human waste were used to fertilize the crops. When we first went to Japan we were afraid to eat any of the Japanese food. In fact we were told, "Don't eat anything. Don't eat any fresh vegetables or fruit because they use human waste for fertilizer." It wasn't processed or anything before it was put out on the fields.

The longer we were there, the more daring we became. We would try this and that. One time several of us had a Sunday off and bicycled to a temple. We were supposed to take a canteen of water with us. We didn't know how far or how

long we would be, so we hadn't taken a canteen that day. The temple had some holy water flowing out of a bamboo pipe. It was nice and clear so we drank some of it. Boy! Did we have a master case of diarrhea after that.

Regardless, I really enjoyed my tour of duty in Japan. I saved my money and bought things to send home to Martha and Janet. I guess Janet still has the Japanese dolls I sent her. I also sent her a little Japanese jacket and Mart took pictures of her wearing it. She always had the jacket on in the pictures my wife sent.

We had a big AP (air policeman) at our base who was the champion of South Japan in boxing. Joe Lewis came over for an exhibition, so we loaded up a plane and visited him in Osaka. The demonstration bout was with our AP. It was held in a nice stadium in Osaka on the island of Honshu.

The air police's big champion was going to spar with Joe Lewis. The two of them got in the ring and the AP thought he was hot stuff and started jabbing Joe pretty hard. Finally Joe gave him one good wham and one heck of a bloody nose. That was the end of that. Joe Lewis was getting pretty old but he had one great punch!

When we had time we would take train rides to different parts of the island of Kyushu where our base was located. We visited a big naval base south of us where a Japanese base had been located. The US Navy was now using the base.

The Japanese also had a cultured pearl farm that we visited. It was interesting. Being a tourist in Japan was really great. I enjoyed getting to see the many places and different sites while getting paid for going there.

I spent 18 months in Japan. They had great beaches and if we were not flying we would go out to the beaches. The water was warm, like Florida. There were also some "Joe-sans" there.

Sometimes, we would ride bicycles out across rice paddies and visit different temples. There were temples all over the place.

During my 18 months stay in Fukuoka, Japan, I was assigned as chief of the support docks. I sent war supplies to Korea. I had seven Japanese working for me who had all been pilots for the Japanese during World War II. There were some that had been majors, colonels and captains. We got along really well. I would teach them English and they would try to teach me Japanese.

The mess for the C-46 crews had a big coffee urn. Usually the mess attendants would pour the leftover coffee out. I would take a big thermos and fill it with the leftover coffee, take it back to the dock, and share it with the Japanese.

Workers from other dock areas would all bring their cups and converge on my dock.

About 00900 all the sergeants would go to the base café and have breakfast. When we returned, all the Japanese were at my dock. The other dock chiefs would cuss me out for stealing their dockworkers. I would rebut, "How could I steal your men when I was with you all the time." The Japanese workers would start laughing and yell "Jotomodgie! Jotomodgie!" I got more work out of the Japanese than anyone else.

In the summer when it was really hot, I would buy a half gallon of ice cream and give it to my dockworkers. The ice cream was made from powdered and canned milk mixed together. It had the canned milk flavor but when it was frozen, it tasted pretty good. I would get the chocolate flavor and that helped to kill the canned milk taste.

When it came time for me to rotate home, all the Japanese workers gave me presents to take home to my "baby-san." There was one older U.S. sergeant that cried when he was sent to Japan, but he had grown to love the Japanese people so much that he cried again when he had to return to the US.

BACK TO THE US

After leaving Japan, I came back through San Francisco, then went home to Bakersfield, California. I was home just long enough to rent out our house and then we departed for Florida and Patrick Air Force Base. When we arrived at the base, housing was still under construction so we had to find housing off base. We found a winter cottage in Melbourne Gardens, just west of

Melbourne. We lived there until the base housing was completed.

One evening, just after work, we could hear a sound that seemed like bull frogs. I *had* to show Janet the bullfrogs. As we started toward the drainage channel, the man that owned the house asked us where we were going. I said that I was going to show Janet the bullfrogs. He exclaimed, "Bull frogs! Hell, that is a mother alligator and her pups. She would eat you alive." We retreated and gave up the idea of seeing frogs.

I was flying C-119s and C-47s down range to the island chains where we had many of our radar tracking stations supporting the firing of our missiles down range from Cape Canaveral. We flew a plane down one day, spent the night at the last island of the chain, and then flew back the next day.

One day one of the planes was on its way back when smoke was detected in the cockpit. The plane was left at the island. The next day, I was chosen to take a pilot and go down to fix the plane and fly it back. Within an hour I had the plane repaired and was airborne flying back to Patrick AFB. After that, I was known as the troubleshooter. When something went bad, they would say, "Send Barnes, he will find it."

Mart, my wife, did not like the thunderstorms and hurricanes in Florida. We lived in a housing facility called "Wherry Housing," which was right on the Atlantic Ocean — the ocean was our backyard. We would go swimming and fishing from our back door. Janet and a neighbor boy were as brown as Mexicans from playing in the sun.

A hurricane came through and the water came over our house. We had to stuff towels and everything in the windows and doorsills to keep the water out. After that, Mart wanted to go back to California. She was really scared.

After serving one more year, I took a discharge and returned to California. This ended my service to my country as a military person. It is a sobering feeling, reviewing my duty to my country, but it gives me great pride knowing that I was a part of what keeps our freedom and liberty together. It also deeply saddens me today to see so many of our leaders and citizens treating those freedoms with so little concern.

Back to Bakersfield again! Mart's father passed away from coal miner's lung.

The Engineering Officer congratulated me and our crew on our good work in Korea. Received an Attaboy Award.

CHAPTER 6

Civilian Once Again ...

NORTH AMERICAN AVIATION AND NASA

I was hired by North American Aircraft Company. The first thing I had to do was look for a hose for my family. I looked around Lancaster, California and couldn't find one that suited Mart. She didn't like cement floors and that was all that was available in Lancaster. Finally, in October of 1954, I found a new, three-bedroom house in Palmdale. We moved to Palmdale and started making ready for a new addition to our family.

Robin joined us on Feb. 19, 1955 and moved into the third bedroom. I had ordered a boy, but nature took control and sent a "tomboy" instead.

At North American, I was first assigned to the X-15 research project being for NASA. I worked for North American for seven years. When the X-15 began the acceptance testing at Edwards Air Force Base, NASA was impressed with my work.

The people at NASA made me a number of offers and finally they made one that I could accept. I lost about 50 cents an hour and the mileage that North American had paid. However, moving over to NASA I was able to use my military service towards retirement. I really enjoyed working there.

THE X-15

The X-15 was the forerunner for the space shuttle. It was launched from a B-52 at high altitude and would fly into the fringes of outer space, then return to Edwards AFB. During re-

entry it does not look like air could do any damage, but it can, and does. If re-entry isn't precisely correct, it can really tear a plane apart.

During one flight, the pilot got the X-15 in a spin at the top of the flight and re-entered the earth's atmosphere backwards. It ripped the wings off the plane and tore it in half. It was incredible to see how badly it was dismantled.

X-15 in flight.

The X-15 was built like a freight train. It was made of Infannal X to withstand the high tem-

As listed, left to right, are Robert D. Rushworth, John McKay, Forest S. Peterson, Joe Walker, Neil Armstrong, Robert W. White. A few of the best X-15 pilots.

peratures, but upon re-entry it just tore the plane into little pieces. NASA flew the plane on 199 flights. To me, as one of the crew chiefs, it was really exciting and I learned a lot.

When there was a known meteorite shower, we would attach little pods to the wing tips. As the X-15 entered the shower, the pilot would open the pods and collect some of the meteorite samples.

NASA had three X-15s. I was crew chief on one. When my plane wasn't flying, a team of us would go to one of the selected dry lake sites as a rescue team. The dry lakes were part of Edwards' extended range that was north along the proposed flight path.

We had a little snub nosed Jeep with a cab over the engine. Since the Jeep was really short, we could put it in a C-130 with a fire truck behind it. The base would fly us up to one of the selected lakes above Reno, Nevada, about two to three hours before a flight.

We would take the Jeep along with our communications radio, put the antenna up, and then wander around the desert, prospecting the hills. By keeping the radio on, we knew when the B-52 was about to launch the X-15. When the B-52

was ready to launch they would be about 50 miles north of our emergency position.

If the X-15 got an engine light and it was okay, everything would go as planned. If the pilot did not get an engine light, he would immediately jettison the fuel and land on the nearest emergency lake, like ours. Our responsibility was to immediately get the pilot out, then purse the X-15 fuel system and prepare the plane to be trucked back to Edwards.

The emergency happened five times. It was a necessary part of each flight to have trained crews stationed along the flight path. After we were dropped off by the C-131, it would return to Edwards, pick up another Jeep and paramedical team and then fly orbit. They would watch and when the X-15 went down, they would drop right down behind the downed pilot and plane to supply any attention that might be required.

The X-15 project lasted 10 years.

LIFTING BODIES AND SPACE SHUTTLES

After the X-15 project came research on lifting bodies for NASA. The lifting bodies designed and tested models for the future space shuttle. The lifting bodies were a wedge shaped configuration that looked like space. The bodies were air lifted to the desired altitude by a B-52

and released. The ride back to the base was no joy ride. Each body was designed to fly without power and dropped at an alarming rate.

Looking back to the beginning of the space program with the first seven astronauts, the step-by-step research for the Space Shuttle was an education all by itself. Much of the testing of the X-15, lifting bodies and many non-flying developments were a part of the many projects that I had the privilege to work on.

The first flight of the shuttle *Columbia* was just a two-astronaut flight from Cape Canaveral with several orbits around our planet to make sure that when the program was fully implemented, everything would be correct and safe. My responsibility with the first flight was the flight landing path guidance system controller. It was part of the ground return system that allowed a glide path for the shuttle to the landing strip on Edwards' dry lake. I cannot express the great feeling we all had as the shuttle came into sight, breaking the sound barrier as it slowed for re-entry. Years of extremely hard work resulted in a perfect flight.

One of the more rewarding parts of the flight was when Bob Crippen and John Young pre-

P r e s e n t e d   t o

CARL C. BARNES

This flag was flown aboard
Space Shuttle **"Columbia"** (STS-1)
April 12 - 14, 1981.
It is presented to you in
recognition of the significant
contribution you made to the
success of the mission.

John Young

Robert Crippen

sented me with a memento of our efforts and first flight. As noted it shows the lift-off from the Cape, the landing at Edwards, and best of all, an American flag that was carried on the flight signed by the two Space Shuttle astronauts.

BLACKBIRDS

My next great thrill was when NASA received several SR-71s, the famous *blackbird* aircraft. I lucked out and became one of the crew chiefs. I was engineering crew chief and was involved in that project for another 10 years. We had a lot of exciting flights with the SR-71s (space boundary, later experiments, high speed friction tests, etc.)

At the conclusion of these flights, NASA put my plane into the museum at Wright Patterson Air Force Research Center. If you should visit the museum, stop and visit my plane #935.

MAKING AVIATION HISTORY

My next assignment was research and development on the KC-135, a winglet program. This project placed winglets on the wing tips, which after our design and tests, resulted in an increase of fuel efficiency of 7%. Commercial and military planes, from small private aircraft to the giant 747, adopted the winglets. Many of the NASA projects I worked on are now part of aviation history. I take a great measure of pride in being a part of this time in our country's efforts to visit space.

Note: During the later part of the KC-135 program, I was under a great deal of pressure that resulted in a mild stroke. I was off work for three months recuperating and trying to regain movement in my left arm. Finally I was able to regain the strength in my arm and go back to work. NASA required a medical physical before they would let me work again.

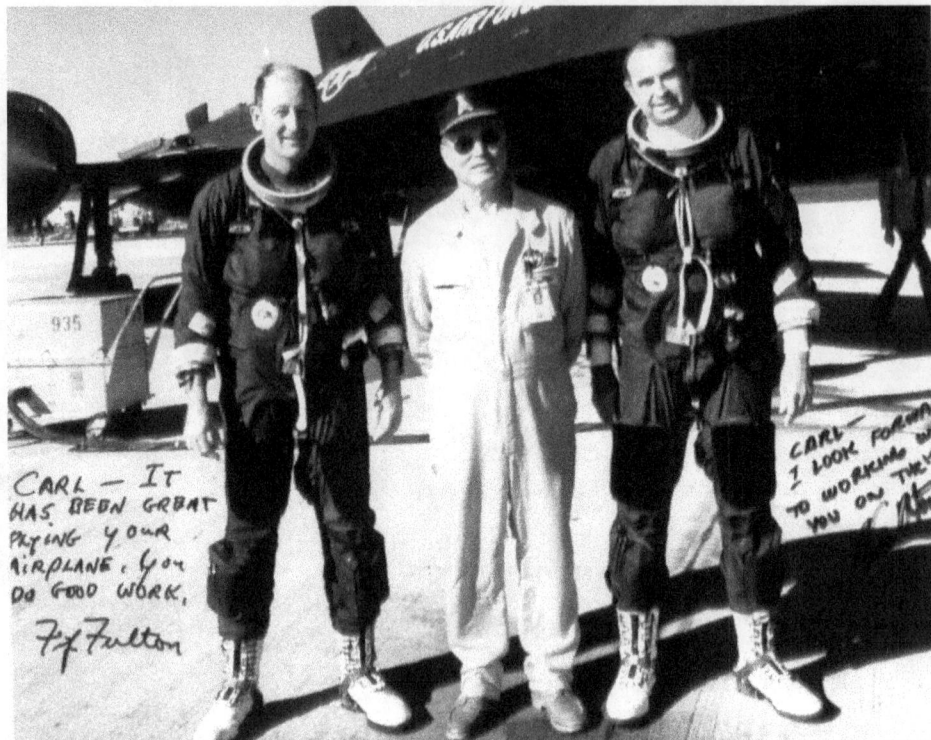

I was okayed to return, but the doctor felt that the stress of the KC-135 was too great so I was given a new project called the AD-1.

THE WATER TUNNEL

One of the most rewarding and interesting projects I worked on was what turned out to be called the *Visualization Flow System*. It was the replacement for the wind tunnel and used water to simulate airflow over any surface. We simply called it the water tunnel.

After engineering reviewed the idea, they asked me if I could build it. It had never been done before and NASA wanted and needed it badly. My response was, "Sure, I can do it." This led to my being transferred to the aerodynamics division in engineering.

Our first objective was to visit the lab at Cal Tech in Pasadena. Cal Tech had developed a horizontal system for the Navy to test and design ship hulls for submarines, torpedoes and other ship designs. The Navy had given Cal Tech the money during WWII. They still had the tunnel available so we reviewed their design and had many long discussions about how it functioned.

Our small group returned to Edwards and began to draw up our own design based upon what was needed. I went to work, sure that I would have one heck of a great system. It took me about a year to complete the project and it worked perfectly.

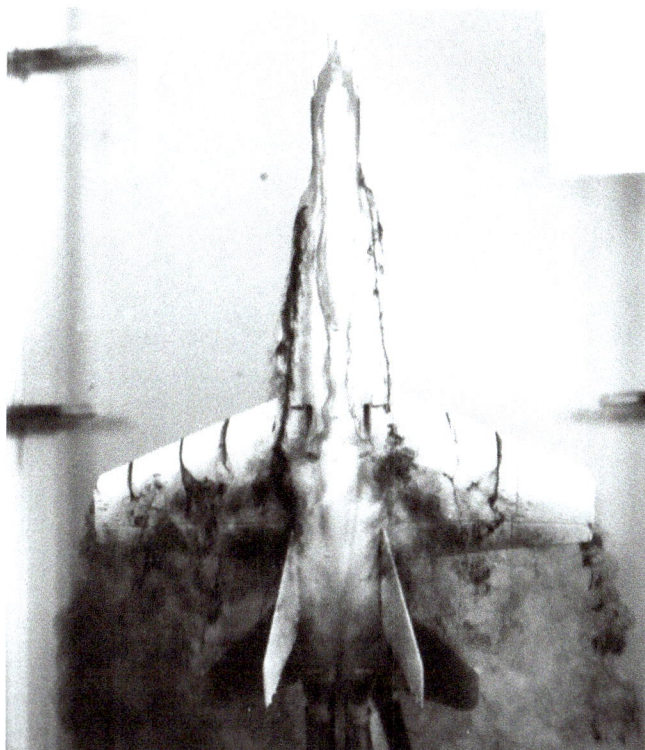

Carl Barnes carving model for visualization tunnel.

Instead of a horizontal bathtub affair, our tunnel was a vertical chamber with highly regulated water flow through the chamber. Any model could be placed in it and the regulated water flow carefully adjusted so that simulation into very high MACH numbers could be obtained. (Water is exactly 2,000 times denser than air).

NASA had many different aircraft companies from all over the country come to visit and use the tunnel. I did research for McDonald Aircraft, Douglas Aircraft, General Dynamics and others, including the F-18 for McDonald Douglas and the F-16 for General Dynamics. Wright Patterson AFB would visit on a regular basis and run different tests like new wing designs and fuselage configurations.

What made the Visualization System so unique was that two video cameras could be focused on the model inside. One from

*Carl Barnes with the **Visualization Flow System** that he constructed to test air flow for NASA*

the front, facing in, and the other from the side. The testing engineer could see double the data from the test being conducted and the "vortex" was clearly displayed in both angles. It was not like instrumentation where it could take weeks before the engineering would have data to evaluate. The water tunnel gave data and results instantly.

I worked on a number of top-secret projects. The companies involved would run tests during weekend visits. I enjoyed that a great deal as I was able to meet a lot of design people, big wheels, and college professors from different colleges all wanting to run tests for their programs. I even ran one for my brother, Art, on his Hyperflow downrigger trolling weights. We bootlegged a lot of fun work for him.

President Reagan visited NASA on one 4th of July. Before he came, the White House Secret Security team came through and checked every

building. They even welded down the manhole covers and closed down many other spaces for security concerns … so that no one could enter the facility.

One day the head of the security team came by the flow system area while checking everything. He started watching a test we were doing. He said, "What are you doing here?" I explained how the system worked by allowing a model to be changed while in the tunnel, showing both the alpha and beta data. This defined any questions concerning vortex or drag from the different surfaces of the model.

I explained that this allowed the engineers to design a plane with the greatest lift, such as the space shuttle, where lift with the correct angle of attack was mandatory for re-entry into the earth's atmosphere. The correct angle kept the shuttle from burning up as it returned to earth.

He thought it was great and he told me, "Carl, you have the most fabulous program here at NASA that I have seen so far." That made me feel great.

A year later, when Reagan was running for his second term, the security chief was in Los Angeles and came by and asked me, "Carl, I have my security team here. Can I bring them in and let them see this flow system? Can you show them how it works?"

I gave a big "Sure."

He brought them in and I really gave them a show, explaining every detail and the purpose of each part of the test being conducted. They thanked me and said it was really educational.

They could see what was going on and understood it. I turned the model in the test chamber so that they could see what a vortex was and explained why it was so important to the design of future aircraft and space shuttles.

I gave them an example. The F-18 had a problem with the tail assembly. In a high maneuver the tail assembly would bend and crack, breaking bolts. The designers needed to know the reason. We made models and began testing them. Immediately we could see the vortex forces off the lexes, right into the vertical tail assembly. Engineering went to work with our data and fixed the problem.

Small doors were cut under the lexest. There was extreme high pressure under them where the jet of air would flow up from the bottom and the small doors would break up the vortex before it hit the vertical assembly. In this manner, we could do quality engineering in a short period of time and at very little cost.

One of the nicer events during my years at NASA was recognition by the top management for some of the outstanding efforts made by employees. Some of them were in letters of commendation for outstanding contributions and others had a little bonus attached.

RECOGNITION

One of the nicer events during my years at NASA was when top management recognized my outstanding efforts. Some of them were in the form of letters of commendation for outstanding contributions and others had a little bonus attached.

I stayed with the *Visualization Flow System* until I retired. After I left NASA, they wanted me back to work in the tunnel. I worked for an independent contractor doing the same work for another five years.

I only worked part time because I was limited to 1,000 hours a year. The extra money allowed me to buy a new pickup and a 5th wheel recreational travel trailer so that Mart and I could really enjoy our hard-earned retirement. We just cruise around visiting some of the better out-of-the way places and our daughter and two grandchildren who live in Northern California.

NATIONAL AERONAUTICS AND SPACE ADMINISTRATION

FLIGHT RESEARCH CENTER
BOX 273. EDWARDS. CALIFORNIA 93523

CLIFFORD 8-3311   TWX: 805-281-5055

IN REPLY REFER TO: 30 July 1964

Mr. Carl C. Barnes
Flight Research Center
Edwards, California

Dear Mr. Barnes:

On February 24, 1964, the National Aeronautics and Space Administration awarded one of its highest awards, the NASA Group Achievement Award, to the X-15 Flight Test Organization. The award was
presented "for outstanding accomplishments during the X-15 Flight
Research Program from its first flight on June 8, 1959 to the one
hundredth flight on January 28, 1964".

It is my pleasure as the Director of the NASA Flight Research
Center to forward a replica of that award to you as a member of
the X-15 flight test organization. Please accept it with my hearti-
est congratulations for your efforts in the program.

                                        Sincerely yours,

                                        Paul F. Bikle
                                        Director

Enc.

NATIONAL AERONAUTICS AND SPACE ADMINISTRATION

FLIGHT RESEARCH CENTER
BOX 273, EDWARDS, CALIFORNIA 93523
CLIFFORD 8-3311   TWX: 805-281-5055

IN REPLY REFER TO:

11 December 64

Mr. Carl C. Barnes
Flight Operations Division
Maintenance & Manufacturing Branch

Dear Mr. Barnes:

It is a distinct pleasure for me to inform you that you have been
awarded $350.00 for Sustained Superior Performance of your duties
for a period of at least six months.

I have been deeply gratified by the outstanding work you have accomplished. In every area of your work you have given unselfishly of
your time and effort. The improvements that have resulted because
of your close attention to your duties reflect great personal credit
on your ability and on your professional knowledge and competence.

I am indeed proud to have this opportunity to congratulate you for
your superior service and contribution to the Flight Research Center.

Sincerely yours,

Paul F. Bikle

Paul F. Bikle
Director

National Aeronautics and
Space Administration

Ames Research Center
Moffett Field, California 94035

(handwritten note): Carl - Thanks for a great effort - It's always especially good to have outside people recognize our capability. Ted Ayers!

Reply to Attn of: RAC: 227-2

TO: Director, Code O/Ames-Dryden Flight Research Facility

FROM: David J. Peake, Chief, Advanced Aerodynamics Concepts Branch

SUBJECT: Letter of Commendation for Carl C. Barnes, Code D-ODTF

I should like to draw to your attention the excellent work that Carl has
done for us recently in designing and building a 1/250-Scale
representation of the 80X120-inlet for testing in the Dryden water tunnel
facility. This has been in association with a directive from
Dr. Ballhaus to me to investigate whether there may be alternatives to
the current plan of modifying the 80x120 inlet of the full-scale
facility. In very short order, Carl developed innovative techniques for
constructing and installing this model in the facility, that included
more than 100 dye ports to visualize the flow within the inlet, and
subsequently, in supporting laser velocimeter measurements. In every
respect, Carl exceeded all expectations of him, working overtime to make
modifications to the rig and to complete tests. His enthusiasum,
willingness and dedication to completing the job in an outstanding
fashion are exemplary and I wanted to ensure that you were made aware of
Carl's superb support for a very important Ames program.

Cordinally Yours,

David J. Peake

cc: Ted G-Ayes, D-O
     Terry Putnam, D-OFA
     Edwin Saltzman, D-OFAA
     Greg Poteat, D-ODTF

DJPeake:ihh 4-22-85/5880

94

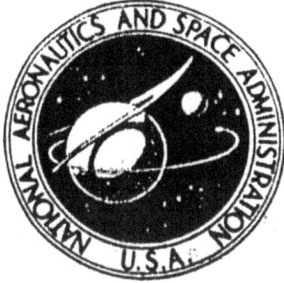

Ames Research Center
Dryden Flight Research Facility

National Aeronautics and Space Administration

presents this

Ames Honor Award

to: CARL C. BARNES

for Excellence in the Category of
TECHNICIAN

JUNE 27, 1985   *Wm F. Bellhouse, Jr.*
Date   Director

The National Aeronautics and Space Administration
Presents the

GROUP ACHIEVEMENT AWARD
to

XV-15 Flight Test Support Team
DRYDEN FLIGHT RESEARCH CENTER

In recognition of an exceptional team effort to establish the critical elements essential to support the Ames XV-15 Tilt Rotor Flight Test Program at Dryden.

Signed and sealed at Washington, DC
this twentieth day of October
Nineteen Hundred and Eighty-One

James M. Beggs
ADMINISTRATOR, NASA

National Aeronautics and Space Administration
Ames/ Dryden Flight Research Facility

Presents the

Group Achievement Award
AFTI/F-111 Loads Laboratory Facility

to

Carl C. Barnes

In recognition of outstanding team effort and excellent support
of the AFTI/F-111 program.

John Manke
_____
Site Manager

December 2, 1982
_____
Date

National Aeronautics and Space Administration
Ames Research Center

Exceptional Performance Award

to

Carl Barnes

In recognition of notable efforts, characterized by outstanding
initiative and ability, resulting in significant contributions to the
successful accomplishment of the Center's missions.

C. A. Syvertson
_____
Director

November 10, 1983
_____
Date

Space Administration

Ames Research Center
Dryden Flight Research Facility
P.O. Box 273
Edwards, California 93523

Reply to Attn of   OFAA/DL   May 3, 1983

To: ODT/Larry Barnett

From: OFA/Chief, Aeronautics Branch

Subject: Constuction of the Dryden Flow
          Visualization Facility (FTF)

The Dryden Flow Visualization Facility (FVF) should prove to be an extremely
useful tool for the Dryden engineering staff. This facility will allow low
cost testing to be performed of many different aerodynamic concepts in a
simple and timely manner. The ability to be able to visualize the aerodynamic flow about an aircraft is extremely important to understanding it's
flying and performance characteristics.

The construction of the FVF involved many individuals from OD that were both
highly capable and motivated. However, one of these fine individuals, Carl
Barnes, stands out as the focal point of the construction. Carl has acted
as the FVF "Crew Chief" since it's inception. His abilities have allowed a
Facility that was really only a concept to become a reality due to his
innovative thinking and his zeal to "get the job done".

During the process of construction of the FVF, many design changes were made
to allow the Facility to have greater capability and reliability. Each of
these design changes were accompanied by many problems that had to be solved
before the Facility could be put into operation. Carl would very often
"engineer" the fixes that were necessary to allow the design changes to be
used.

Carl Barnes, and the other indiviuals in your oganization like him, is truly
an asset to the Dryden Facility. We of the engineering staff truly
appreciate the work of this fine individual.

Terrell W. Putnam

cc:
OF/K. J. Szalai
O/J. A. Manke
OD/R. S. Waite
ODT/L. C. Barnett

25th Anniversary
1958-1983

97

National Aeronautics and
Space Administration

Ames Research Center
Moffett Field, California 94035

APT:241-3   August 15, 1983

Mr. Carl C. Barnes
Dryden Flight Research Facility
P.O. Box 273
Edwards, CA 93523

Dear Carl:

Ames-North and Ames-Dryden have a number of missions in several fields
of importance to the nation's welfare. Our work is, therefore, significant
to us not only as members of the Ames-Dryden but also as citizens. Employees
such as yourself have made many contributions to the efficient operation
of the facility.

I would like to take this opportunity to commend you for the exceptionally
high quality of your work. You have exceeded the standards set for your
position and your dedication to duty and superior performance have long
been recognized by your associates.

On behalf of your supervisor, it is my pleasure to inform you that you
have been recommended for a NASA Special Achievement Award. This letter
and the enclosed check are tokens of our appreciation for your contribution
to the Ames-Dryden's accomplishments.

Sincerely,

C. A. Syvertson
Director

Enclosure

EIDETICS
INTERNATIONAL

November 22, 1985

Mr. Ted Ayers
Deputy Director
Flight Operations and Research
NASA Dryden Flight Research Facility
Edwards AFB, CA 93523

Carl,
It's always great to hear
from people who have had
a good experience at Dryden.
You certainly made an
impression on Jerry. Thanks for
the good work.
Ted Ayers

Dear Ted:

As you are aware, I spent two weeks at your facility recently to conduct
some basic research experiments in your water tunnel flow visualization facility
to study some concepts for vortex control on a generic fighter model for
AFWAL. I want to take this opportunity to express my appreciation for not
only allowing us but encouraging us to use your very fine facility for this
study. From the day of my first contact with Larry Montoya to the day I
finished my experiments I always had the full cooperation and help from your
people. I especially want to thank John Del Frate and Carl Barns for their
daily assistance and advice during the tests and to acknowledge the very
significant contribution of Carl to the success of these experiments. His
knowledge and skill in operating the tunnel and his friendly and patient
assistance were important factors.

This facility is an important asset to NASA Dryden, and making it available
to outside users is a very valuable and significant contribution to encouraging
innovation and evaluation of new ideas.

I look forward to sharing the results of this study with you and to the possibility
of working with my former colleagues at NASA again.

Sincerely,

Gerald Malcolm
Director, Research and Technology
Eidetics International

GM:flh

Veterans of Foreign Wars

of the United States

Presented To

Carl C. Barnes

For Meritorious and Distinguished Service in Furthering the Aims and Ideals of the Veterans of Foreign Wars of the United States.

Given this 21ST day of May 1992

Commander *Phillip A. Conwell*

Adjutant *Frank Alex*

Veterans of Foreign Wars
of the United States

Presented To

Carl C. Barnes

For Meritorious and Distinguished
Service in Furthering the Aims and
Ideals of the Veterans of Foreign
Wars of the United States.

Given this **20th** day of **May** 19**93**

Commander *Paul E. Goins*

Adjutant *Frank Ley*

CONCLUSION

Conclusion means the end of something. There can never be an end to the memory of the 50,000+ most heroic airmen who never returned to their families and friends.

Some 50 years and more after their sacrifice, our country has seen several more conflicts that were labeled "Police Actions" where, again, our very best young patriotic men and women answered the call of duty for our country and died defending the ideals that have kept us free. Many have questioned the loss of so many in foreign conflicts that seemed to not have a direct value for our country.

Let just one of the dissenters of today lose their liberty and freedom in our country and the cry would be, "Where is our military?" Each one of our countrymen and women who have felt the call of Duty, Honor and Country in their bones needs to stand up and honor all the service persons who have paid the ultimate price so that we, in this very troubling world who cherish that liberty and freedom can continue for all times.

Carl Columbus Barnes
MARCH 10, 1921–JANUARY 6, 2003

Bibliography

Valor at Polebrook, Rick School/Jeff Rodgers

Combat Crew, John Comer

The Mighty Eighth, Janes, Rodger Freeman

Polbrook Post, 351st Bomb Group Association, 508th, 509th, 510th, 511th

A number of newspaper articles and internet sites.

Special Thanks

Most importantly for their contributions, thanks go to several friends who were flying over Germany during the time of the referenced events.

To my brother, Carl, who after the many wonderful hours of my threatening him finally decided to share his duty, honor and country contributions with me and you.

There is no greater love —AHB